DAILY-WEEKLY

The Letters to the Thessalonians

Matt O'Reilly

Cover design by Strange Last Name
Page design by PerfecType, Nashville, Tennessee

O'Reilly, Matt, Dr.
  The letters to the Thessalonians / Matt O'Reilly. – Franklin, Tennessee : Seedbed Publishing, ©2020.

      pages ; cm. + 1 videodisc – (OneBook. Daily-weekly)

      ISBN 9781628247459 (pbk. : alk. paper)
      ISBN 9781628247497 (DVD)
      ISBN 9781628247466 (mobipocket ebk.)
      ISBN 9781628247473 (epub ebk.)
      ISBN 9781628247480 (updf ebk.)

      1. Bible. Thessalonians -- Textbooks. 2. Bible. Thessalonians -- Study and teaching.
      3. Bible. Thessalonians -- Commentaries.   I. Title. II. Series.

BS2725.55.O73 2019   227/.81   2020931231

 Seedbed

SEEDBED PUBLISHING
Franklin, Tennessee
seedbed.com

CONTENTS

Contents

Week Four

Holy Bodies, New Bodies   34
(1 Thessalonians 4:1–18)

Week Five

Standing Firm, Becoming Holy   45
(1 Thessalonians 5:1–28)

Week Six

Your Journey toward Glory   56
(2 Thessalonians 1:1–12)

Contents

Week Seven

What Happens Next?   67

(2 Thessalonians 2:1–17)

Week Eight

Wrapping Up   78

(2 Thessalonians 3:1–18)

WELCOME TO ONEBOOK DAILY-WEEKLY

John Wesley, in a letter to one of his leaders, penned the following:

> O begin! Fix some part of every day for private exercises. You may acquire the taste which you have not: what is tedious at first, will afterwards be pleasant. Whether you like it or not, read and pray daily. It is for your life; there is no other way; else you will be a trifler all your days. . . . Do justice to your own soul; give it time and means to grow. Do not starve yourself any longer. Take up your cross and be a Christian altogether.

Rarely are our lives most shaped by our biggest ambitions and highest aspirations. Rather, our lives are most shaped, for better or for worse, by those small things we do every single day.

At Seedbed, our biggest ambition and highest aspiration is to resource the followers of Jesus to become lovers and doers of the Word of God every single day, to become people of One Book.

To that end, we have created the OneBook Daily-Weekly. First, it's important to understand what this is not: warm, fuzzy, sentimental devotions. If you engage the Daily-Weekly for any length of time, you will learn the Word of God. You will grow profoundly in your love for God, and you will become a passionate lover of people.

How Does the Daily-Weekly Work?

Daily. As the name implies, every day invites a short but substantive engagement with the Bible. Five days a week you will read a passage of Scripture followed by a short segment of teaching and closing with questions for reflection and self-examination. On the sixth day, you will review and reflect on the previous five days.

Weekly. Each week, on the seventh day, find a way to gather with at least one other person doing the study. Pursue the weekly guidance for gathering. Share learning, insight, encouragement, and most important, how the Holy Spirit is working in your lives.

That's it. Depending on the length of the study, when the eight or twelve weeks are done, we will be ready with the next study. On an ongoing basis, we will release new editions of the Daily-Weekly. Over time, those who pursue this course of learning will develop a rich library of Bible learning resources for the long haul.

OneBook Daily-Weekly will develop eight- and twelve-week studies that cover the entire Old and New Testaments. Seedbed will publish new studies regularly so that an ongoing supply of group lessons will be available. All titles will remain accessible, which means they can be used in any order that fits your needs or the needs of your group.

If you are looking for a substantive study to learn Scripture through a steadfast method, look no further.

WEEK ONE

1 Thessalonians 1:1–10

Unexpected News, New Community

ONE

Faith, Love, Hope

1 Thessalonians 1:1–3 *Paul, Silvanus, and Timothy, To the church of the Thessalonians in God the Father and the Lord Jesus Christ: Grace to you and peace.*

²We always give thanks to God for all of you and mention you in our prayers, constantly ³remembering before our God and Father your work of faith and labor of love and steadfastness of hope in our Lord Jesus Christ.

Key Observation. All followers of Jesus are called to be in active ministry, not just pastors and church staff.

Understanding the Word. Few people write letters anymore. For a long time, letters were the only way to communicate long distance. People didn't have phones. Or e-mail. Or texting. In the ancient Greek-speaking world, letters followed a pattern. The author put his or her name at the top followed by the recipient. Then came a word of greeting. This letter is addressed to the whole congregation, not one individual. It's meant for the whole group. That means it isn't just a letter, it's also a speech. And when it arrived, someone would've read it to the whole congregation. These opening verses hint at what Paul finds most important: faith, love, and hope. Those three virtues will keep coming up.

This first mention of faith, love, and hope comes in a prayer. We might be tempted to hurry on to the meat of the letter, but I've learned that when Paul prays, it's worth slowing down and lingering. Let's hear what he says. First,

Paul's prayer reminds the Thessalonians of their importance to him. He intercedes for them. He thanks God for them. He does it *always* and *constantly*. You feel his affection for them. They'll want to hear what he says, because they know how much he cares.

Second, what does work have to do with faith, labor with love, and steadfastness with hope? For Paul, virtue produces action—faith produces work; love produces labor; hope produces perseverance. What's the difference between *work* and *labor*? Both words describe the mission of the church. In 1 Thessalonians 2:9, Paul mentions his own labor and work in gospel ministry. The same pair of words designate his work and the Thessalonians' work. Here's why that matters. Paul is depicting the Thessalonians as participants in the mission. They labor with him; they work with him. That work flows out of their faith and love. There is no hint that Paul is a professional hired to do ministry for the congregation. Forget that. Paul wants his first hearers to know—and he wants us to know—that the whole community of believers, both leaders and congregation, participate together in God's mission to bring the good news of King Jesus to the world.

The continued success of that mission requires steadfast endurance, and endurance flows out of hope in Jesus. We'll find out later in the letter that life hasn't been easy for the Thessalonians. They've suffered for following Jesus. But they've stayed on course despite adversity. Paul will say more about that later. The main thing to discover here is that God gives the strength to stay faithful to the mission, especially when it's hard.

1. Think of a time when you suffered or had a setback. What was the cause? Did you have a community of believers to help you through that time? How did you handle it? What was the outcome?

2. How have you labored in mission with your community of faith? What is God calling you to do next?

3. What are you doing to strengthen your partnership with other believers to advance the kingdom of God?

TWO

Gospel Power

1 Thessalonians 1:4–5 *For we know, brothers and sisters beloved by God, that he has chosen you, ⁵because our message of the gospel came to you not in word only, but also in power and in the Holy Spirit and with full conviction; just as you know what kind of persons we proved to be among you for your sake.*

Key Observation. When we tell the story of Jesus' death and resurrection, the Holy Spirit uses our words to convict people of sin and bring them into a relationship of life-giving love with God.

Understanding the Word. Why was Paul so deeply committed to the gospel? We're about to find out. Now *gospel* is a word that means good news. In ancient Rome, it was used to celebrate the reign of a new emperor or a major military victory. But when Paul spoke of the gospel, he was referring to the story of Jesus. It's the good news that Jesus of Nazareth died to rescue people from the consequences and power of sin. It's the good news that Jesus was raised bodily from the dead. And it's the good news that Jesus has been exalted to the throne of heaven where he reigns over the cosmos, everything that has been made, whether we can see it or not.

Paul knows this gospel has unique power. This good news is unlike other news. These words are unlike any other words. Why? The answer comes in three parts: power, Holy Spirit, conviction. When Paul told the story of Jesus, people weren't simply persuaded by good arguments; God's Holy Spirit transformed them. It may help to remember how strange the Jesus story must have sounded in first-century Thessalonica. Paul spoke of a Jewish man named Jesus who was crucified as a failed revolutionary, then raised bodily from the dead, and exalted to the throne of heaven. He had to know how unlikely it would be for people to believe that. Nevertheless, Paul was gripped by the gospel. He had to tell the story. And as he told the story, he found others were gripped too. They believed what Paul said about Jesus. They trusted. They obeyed. There was new power at work in them—the power of God's Holy Spirit.

And what does the Spirit do? The Spirit brings full conviction. Take a minute to think of a time you did something wrong. Did you feel bad about it? That feeling is used by the Holy Spirit to persuade us of our sin. That's the negative aspect of conviction, and it's an essential step toward making things right. More positively, however, conviction can also describe strong beliefs. When we embrace the truth of the gospel and become fully committed to it, we call it a conviction. We may even call it *deep* conviction. Paul probably has both meanings in mind. When the good news about Jesus is told, God's Spirit opens our eyes to things that keep us from knowing God (we can call those things sin) and persuades us of the truth about Jesus. That's what Paul means by "full conviction." That's what the Holy Spirit does when God's people tell the Jesus story.

1. Can you think of time when you experienced God's grace before you became a follower of Jesus? Why is it important to know that salvation is always initiated by God through the Holy Spirit?

2. Have you ever had the experience to share the good news about Jesus with another person? How did you feel? What did you do?

3. What can you do to create more opportunities to talk about Jesus with new people? How can your community help you?

THREE
Life Worth Imitating

1 Thessalonians 1:6–8 *And you became imitators of us and of the Lord, for in spite of persecution you received the word with joy inspired by the Holy Spirit, [7]so that you became an example to all the believers in Macedonia and in Achaia. [8]For the word of the Lord has sounded forth from you not only in Macedonia and Achaia, but in every place your faith in God has become known, so that we have no need to speak about it.*

Key Observation. God's kingdom spreads when believers live in a manner worthy of imitation. Less self centered

Understanding the Word. Have you noticed how passion is contagious? If you've ever had a teacher who loves her subject and her students, you know what I mean. You can't help but share the excitement; the passion rubs off. That's what it was like when Paul got to Thessalonica. He was nothing if not passionate. Remember Paul sacrificed an upwardly mobile and influential life to become a traveling church planter. He was dedicated to the mission. His love for Jesus rubbed off on the Thessalonians. They became imitators of Paul.

Now this is the first time in the letter Paul mentions how the Thessalonians endured persecution. He doesn't go into detail, but he does connect their perseverance to imitation. Like Paul, they remained faithful despite the cost. Ultimately, imitation is about Jesus, who suffered and died to redeem us. Jesus wasn't focused on his own needs or comfort. He didn't prioritize the preservation of his life; he prioritized the salvation of the world. He "emptied himself of all but love," as one songwriter put it.[1] All Christian imitation boils down to imitating the self-giving love of Jesus. That's a life worth imitating. Paul imitated Jesus. The Thessalonians imitated Paul.

Now if we're going to talk about imitation, there are two concepts to cover: transformation and multiplication. Let's take transformation first. When Paul says the Thessalonians "became imitators" of him, he implies that their lives changed. The Thessalonians had to be willing to look at themselves and determine what didn't line up with God's best. Whether it's idolatry, anger, laziness, or something else, following Jesus means some things stop and other things start. How do we know what to stop doing and what to start doing? God gives us people to imitate. The Thessalonians looked at Paul as an example of commitment to Jesus. He taught them how to be single-minded, devoted, and holy. He lived a life worth imitating, and his life was an instrument of grace to the Thessalonians. In Paul, they saw a real difference.

What's striking is that the process didn't stop when the Thessalonians became imitators of Paul. As they changed, they also became an example for others to imitate. Their reputation spread to the north (Macedonia) and the south (Achaia). That's what I mean by multiplication. If one believer lives a life worth imitating, and a few people begin to imitate him or her and others begin to imitate them, then the number of people who embody the character of Jesus grows. Imitation is how the world changes.

---

1. Charles Wesley, "And Can It Be, That I Should Gain?" 1738. Public domain.

5

I hope you are beginning to see that Christian community is essential. If we think of Christianity as a solo project—a private relationship between me and Jesus that doesn't depend on others—then there is no place for imitation. If we are going to imitate someone, then we need to be in community with that person. And if others are going to imitate us, the same is true. Imitation requires community.

1. Think of a time when you experienced a challenge or setback. How did you respond? Would you respond differently now that you know imitation of Jesus involves perseverance through suffering?

2. Do you have mature followers of Jesus to imitate? Who are they? Do you live in a way that is worthy of imitation? Could you tell a new follower of Jesus, "Imitate me as I imitate Christ"?

3. What changes do you need to make to begin to live a life worthy of imitation?

FOUR
Gotta Serve Someone

1 Thessalonians 1:9–10 *For the people of those regions report about us what kind of welcome we had among you, and how you turned to God from idols, to serve a living and true God, ¹⁰and to wait for his Son from heaven, whom he raised from the dead—Jesus, who rescues us from the wrath that is coming.*

Key Observation. An idol is anything that gets more of our energy and devotion than Jesus. Following Jesus means turning from idols.

Understanding the Word. People are starting to talk. The Thessalonians are getting a reputation. And Paul couldn't be happier. They've turned from idols to worship the true God. Now the Roman Empire had no shortage of gods and no shortage of shrines to honor those gods. There were the typical gods from Greek and Roman mythology. You may have heard of Zeus or Poseidon or Athena or Aphrodite. And there were others. Some of the emperors were even worshipped as deities. And the Romans didn't separate devotion from business, family, or fun. To the contrary, worship was interwoven with every facet of life. Pagan piety permeated Roman society. This may explain why the Thessalonians faced persecution. When they stopped revering the Roman gods, it would have been perceived as a threat to society. In contrast, Jewish people like Paul believed there was nothing to pagan idols. Those gods were false gods; idols were just carved wood and metal. The true God is the living Creator. He requires his people to worship him alone (see Exodus 20:1–4).

Now most of us probably don't have statues in our homes that we bow to every day. But what if idolatry (the worship of false gods) has less to do with carved statues and more to do with our values and priorities? Who gets our best? How do we spend our energy? Our time? Our money? How do we use our resources? What do we care about most? If we want to know what we worship, those are the questions to ask.

Framed this way, all sorts of things (other than God) become candidates for our worship. Am I a workaholic? Do I neglect my faith and my family to climb the corporate ladder? And what about entertainment? Do I spend excessive money on stuff that I think will make me happy? Houses? Cars? Televisions? Game systems? Ever consider how easy it is to be more devoted to a college football team than to the kingdom of God? And what happens when we let our kids prioritize athletics or other activities over the worship of God and the mission of the church? What are we teaching our children when other things (like a Little League game) keep us from gathering with other believers to worship Jesus, who loved us and gave himself for us? Our kids know who our gods are.

Paul wants his readers to understand that the worship of the one true God revealed in Jesus is mutually exclusive with the worship of other things. We can't do both. We'll either worship God or we'll worship something else. That's why Paul talks about turning from idols to God. The Thessalonians had to turn their backs on the false gods of Rome to become followers of Jesus. And we have to do the same with our idols. Now I'm not saying you can't ever go to a ball game again. And I'm not saying you shouldn't have a car or go to the movies. I'm inviting you to think about who or what gets your best. Is it Jesus? Or something else?

1. Take a minute to consider your priorities. Who or what gets most of your energy and attention?

2. What idols do you need to turn from? How can group members help each other make that turn?

FIVE

Why Wrath?

1 Thessalonians 1:9–10 *For the people of those regions report about us what kind of welcome we had among you, and how you turned to God from idols, to serve a living and true God, ¹⁰and to wait for his Son from heaven, whom he raised from the dead—Jesus, who rescues us from the wrath that is coming.*

Key Observation. God's wrath is his measured, intentional, holy, and just opposition to forces that destroy his good creation.

Understanding the Word. There's something we need to admit up front. A lot of people struggle with the Bible's talk of God's wrath. We find the idea of an angry deity uncomfortable and off-putting. Who wants to worship a God like that? We'd much rather hear about God's love than God's wrath. So, what do we do with passages like this?

What if I told you God's wrath is necessary because of God's love? Think about it this way. Love is at the heart of God's character. God loves the world. He made it; it's his. And God loves human beings. He made us to embody the beauty of the glory of his image and he has graciously called us to represent him to the world. But there's an enemy out there. And that enemy is committed to destroying God's beautiful creation. The enemy is sin. It's a cancer that corrupts human life. It moves people to vanity, to strive for selfish gain, to manipulate the world, and to use God's good creation for their own evil ends. Now if God is committed to his creation, and if there's an enemy bent on destroying that creation, what posture do you think God will take toward that enemy? The answer should be clear: he'll go after it with everything he's got; he'll show that enemy no mercy. And he'll do it because he loves his world. He'll do it because he loves us.

That's what Paul means by the wrath of God. We're uncomfortable with that language because we've all seen or experienced unholy human wrath: an abusive husband or father, a vicious colleague, oppressive dictators, merciless terrorists. When we hear of *divine* wrath, we take those wicked examples and maximize them by infinite proportion. But that isn't what Paul means. God's wrath is not the fury of an angry father or the mad aspirations of a power-hungry tyrant. (God's wrath is his opposition to anything that harms his good creation. It's measured and intentional. It's right and just—holy and good. And it's the result of his love. God loves us. That's why he turns his wrath on sin, because sin attempts to destroy everything God loves.)

The problem is that people dig in their heels and refuse to break their alliance with sin. They are committed to the corrupting cancerous power of sin. They don't want to be free from it. They give themselves to it. And they love it. Paul preached that Jesus died and was raised to set us free from sin. Jesus gave everything to disentangle us from that which seeks to destroy us. God will put everything right. That's what we're waiting for.

But waiting doesn't mean passivity. Paul doesn't expect believers to hang out and do nothing until God wraps up the project. Waiting for Jesus means actively working to advance his kingdom, engaging in mission, proclaiming the good news, and opposing evil in every form. That's what Paul calls the Thessalonians to do. That's what Jesus calls us all to do.

1. Think of a time you saw or experienced human wrath. How is God's just opposition against sin different from that?

2. What is your community doing to resist the evil in the world as you eagerly await Jesus' return?

Vote

9

WEEK ONE

GATHERING DISCUSSION OUTLINE

A. **Open session in prayer.** Ask that God would astonish us anew with fresh insight from God's Word and transform us into the disciples that Jesus desires us to become.

B. **View video for this week's readings.**

C. **What were key insights or takeaways that you gained from your reading during the week and from watching the video commentary?** In particular, how did these help you to grow in your faith and understanding of Scripture this week? What parts of the Bible lessons or study raised questions for you?

D. **Discuss questions selected from the daily readings.** Invite class members to share key insights or to raise questions that they found to be the most meaningful.

   1. **KEY OBSERVATION:** All followers of Jesus are called to be in active ministry, not just pastors and church staff.

     DISCUSSION QUESTION: What are you doing to strengthen your partnership with other believers to advance the kingdom of God?

   2. **KEY OBSERVATION:** When we tell the story of Jesus' death and resurrection, the Holy Spirit uses our words to convict people of sin and bring them into a relationship of life-giving love with God.

     DISCUSSION QUESTION: What can you do to create more opportunities to talk about Jesus with new people? How can your community help you?

3. **KEY OBSERVATION:** God's kingdom spreads when believers live in a manner worthy of imitation.

   DISCUSSION QUESTION: What changes do you need to make to begin to live a life worthy of imitation?

4. **KEY OBSERVATION:** An idol is anything that gets more of our energy and devotion than Jesus. Following Jesus means turning from idols.

   DISCUSSION QUESTION: What idols do you need to turn from? How can group members help each other make that turn?

5. **KEY OBSERVATION:** God's wrath is his measured, intentional, holy, and just opposition to forces that destroy his good creation.

   DISCUSSION QUESTION: What is your community doing to resist the evil in the world as you eagerly await Jesus' return?

E. **As the study concludes, consider specific ways that this week's Bible lessons invite you to grow and call you to change.** How do this week's scriptures call us to think differently? How do they challenge us to change in order to align ourselves with God's work in the world? What specific actions should we take to apply the insights of the lessons into our daily lives? What kind of person do our Bible lessons call us to become?

F. **Close session with prayer.** Emphasize God's ongoing work of transformation in our lives in preparation for loving mission and service in the world. Pray for absent class members as well as for persons whom we need to invite to join our study.

WEEK TWO

1 Thessalonians 2:1–20

Shared Suffering, Shared Life

ONE

People-Pleaser or God-Pleaser?

1 Thessalonians 2:1–8 NIV *You know, brothers and sisters, that our visit to you was not without results. ²We had previously suffered and been treated outrageously in Philippi, as you know, but with the help of our God we dared to tell you his gospel in the face of strong opposition. ³For the appeal we make does not spring from error or impure motives, nor are we trying to trick you. ⁴On the contrary, we speak as those approved by God to be entrusted with the gospel. We are not trying to please people but God, who tests our hearts. ⁵You know we never used flattery, nor did we put on a mask to cover up greed—God is our witness. ⁶We were not looking for praise from people, not from you or anyone else, even though as apostles of Christ we could have asserted our authority. ⁷Instead, we were like young children among you.*

Just as a nursing mother cares for her children, ⁸so we cared for you. Because we loved you so much, we were delighted to share with you not only the gospel of God but our lives as well.

Key Observation. All of life should be lived to please God alone.

Understanding the Word. Most of us live under constant pressure to please people. Employers, coworkers, our spouse, friends, church members—we want others to be happy with us. That desire is reinforced by constant immersion in social media, which always leaves us craving one more "like." Paul

being gentle gains respect

offers a vision of Christian life that is radically countercultural. He doesn't live to please people. Paul lives to please God. That's the focus of 1 Thessalonians 2, and it has big implications for Paul and us.

First, living to please God meant Paul would suffer. His message about Jesus faced opposition. He mentions they had "suffered and been treated outrageously" in Philippi. We learn in Acts 16 that Paul was accused of disturbing the city and encouraging illegal activity. So, the city authorities had him stripped, beaten, and jailed. But Paul didn't live to please them; he lived to please God. And God called Paul to preach Jesus. Paul lived courageously into his calling, despite the suffering.

We don't always think of following Jesus as something that takes courage. In North America, we aren't in danger of being arrested for going to church. We can follow Jesus without fear of physical harm. But there are places in the world where following Jesus does take courage—great courage. In some parts of China, people who become Christians risk being disowned by family or reported to the local government. Evangelism was recently criminalized in Bolivia. If you attempt to lead someone to Jesus in that country, you could be imprisoned for five to twelve years. It takes real courage to follow Jesus in places like that.

Second, living to please God motivates integrity. All of us can think of preachers who are known as tricksters. They promise health and wealth to those who give money to their ministries, and they end up looking like they're in it for the money. Paul doesn't want to give that impression. He's not preaching for the payoff. He's not doing it for public acclaim. He's not out to be a celebrity. He simply wants to be faithful. You see, Paul understood that our lives will either commend the gospel or undermine it. If we're going to tell people Jesus loves them, we need to also embody that love. If we appear to seek our own gain, we hinder the gospel and create barriers to faith for others. Living to please God means living with integrity that commends the good news.

1. Imagine God is calling you to be a missionary in a country where Christians are persecuted. What emotions would you experience? Would your family and friends encourage you or discourage you from living to please God? How would you respond?

a little fearful, but if God himself
called me, I would have to go

13

2. Think of a time someone's behavior undermined their Christian witness. What could they have done to strengthen their witness instead? What are one or two specific things you can do that will commend the good news to others?

3. What areas in your life are lived to please someone other than God?

sometimes social, friends family work

TWO

When Life Gets Hard

1 Thessalonians 2:7–12 NIV *Instead, we were like young children among you. Just as a nursing mother cares for her children, *[8]*so we cared for you. Because we loved you so much, we were delighted to share with you not only the gospel of God but our lives as well. *[9]*Surely you remember, brothers and sisters, our toil and hardship; we worked night and day in order not to be a burden to anyone while we preached the gospel of God to you. *[10]*You are witnesses, and so is God, of how holy, righteous and blameless we were among you who believed. *[11]*For you know that we dealt with each of you as a father deals with his own children, *[12]*encouraging, comforting and urging you to live lives worthy of God, who calls you into his kingdom and glory.*

Key Observation. Christian community should be characterized by self-giving love, even in difficult circumstances.

Understanding the Word. Life has likely presented you with undesirable circumstances at least once or twice and probably more. Perhaps you've lost a job or there has been conflict at church. Maybe you're grieving over a broken friendship or the loss of a loved one. Whatever the situation, it's easy to stress when things get painful. We focus on ourselves, on getting through, on self-preservation. Paul could have done that. After all, he'd been treated with violence for preaching Jesus. It would have been easy to pity himself. But instead of focusing on his own painful circumstances, he focused on the Thessalonians and their needs. He offered himself to them. He didn't show up expecting recognition or support. He didn't ask them to carry his burdens. Paul's reminder that he could have "asserted our authority" (2:6 NIV) suggests that his role as an apostle entitled him to some provision. But he didn't insist

He didn't show up for a pat on his back

14

on his rights. He came alongside the Thessalonians and cared for them. The images of nursemaid and mother combine to magnify the depth of Paul's love. He wanted to please God; he gave himself to others despite his pain.

Paul's behavior is an example for the Thessalonians and for us. And he knows it. That's why he encourages them to "live lives worthy of God." He's not simply reminding them about his self-sacrificing love; he wants them to act the same way. We learned in chapter 1 that the Thessalonians had experienced persecution (1:6). Paul's ministry shows how to respond to that. Whatever they suffered, they had to resist the temptation to turn their attention to themselves. If they did, one of two things would probably happen. First option, the church could become a holy huddle with members focused on maintaining themselves while giving little or no attention to mission and the growth of the kingdom. If they go this route, the church becomes something that exists only to meet their needs. And they become consumers who only show up for what they can get. It would be easy to shift into survival mode, but it would also be detrimental to the community. Second option, they turn on each other. When things get tough, it's easy to play the blame game. This creates strife and division, and it tears churches apart.

Paul prefers a third option. He wants to see a community characterized by self-giving love. And he's doing his best to model that. If that's what we want, we can't come together to blame or consume. We come to give and serve. We come to cultivate our shared mission. If we do that, then we'll begin to understand what Paul means when he talks about holiness later in the letter. It's been said that sin is a human heart turned in on itself. In contrast, the holy life—the life worthy of God—is a life marked by self-giving love oriented toward others. It's a life that embodies the character of God revealed in the self-sacrificial love of Jesus. It's a life that only comes with the gracious presence of the Holy Spirit. And as we'll see later, it's God's will for everyone (see 1 Thessalonians 4:3).

1. What's your attitude toward church? Do you go for what you get or for what you give?

2. What's one area of life in which you need to turn from focus on self to focus on others?

3. What are two or three specific things you can do to cultivate self-giving love in your community?

volunteer
help others

THREE

But How?

1 Thessalonians 2:13–14a NIV *And we also thank God continually because, when you received the word of God, which you heard from us, you accepted it not as a human word, but as it actually is, the word of God, which is indeed at work in you who believe. ¹⁴For you, brothers and sisters, became imitators of God's churches in Judea, which are in Christ Jesus . . .*

Key Observation. Faith is trusting God to do what we cannot do for ourselves.

Understanding the Word. So how do you do it? How do you find the strength to give yourself in love to others, especially if you're suffering? How do you live a worthy life pleasing to God?

For Paul, the power to live in a manner worthy of God doesn't come from our ability, ingenuity, intellect, or strength. It comes when God's power goes to work in us. How does that happen? The answer comes in a word that's used so often in so many different ways that it has nearly lost its meaning. So, it's worth a few minutes to sort out what Paul does and doesn't mean when he uses this word. The word is *faith*. We know that's what Paul has in mind because he mentions how God's power is at work in "believers." Paul wrote in Greek, and the English words *faith* and *belief* are translations of the same Greek word. Paul is saying: God's Word is at work "in you who have faith." This question gets to the point: If God's power works on the condition of our faith, how do we cultivate that specific sort of faith?

Now sometimes people talk about faith like it's a work to earn God's favor. You've heard this. It usually comes in two parts: (1) if you're suffering, then it means you don't have enough faith; (2) if you believe harder, then you'll prosper. Sometimes this message is called the "health and wealth gospel" or the "prosperity gospel." Every time I hear it, I can't help but think of all the suffering Paul endured to spread the gospel and plant churches. You can be sure that Paul didn't suffer because he lacked faith. The opposite is true. He was willing to endure great suffering precisely because he trusted God to sustain him. If there's one thing we learn from Paul, it's that faithfulness may involve great pain.

That brings us to the heart of Paul's understanding of faith—*trust*. Do I *It's* trust God to do for me what I can't do for myself? Do I trust God to sustain *hard* me? To care for me when I suffer? To strengthen me when I'm weak? That's what it means to *receive* and *accept* God's Word. Faith isn't work that earns God's favor. Faith accepts the reality that God must do what we cannot.

It's also common for people to think of faith as something that happens spiritually on the inside but doesn't ultimately have to do with outward behavior. Paul won't let us go there either. The faith of the Thessalonians led them to imitate the believers in Judea who were faithful despite persecution. Faith is not a work of self-sufficiency, but it does produce faithful work. That's why faith is vital to a life that pleases God.

1. Think of a time when you suffered. Did you trust God? If so, how did that trust change your experience? If not, why?

2. How can you begin to trust God more in those areas of life in which you are self-reliant?

FOUR

Where Is God?

1 Thessalonians 2:14b–16 NIV . . . *You suffered from your own people the same things those churches suffered from the Jews* [15]*who killed the Lord Jesus and the prophets and also drove us out. They displease God and are hostile to everyone* [16]*in their effort to keep us from speaking to the Gentiles so that they may be saved. In this way they always heap up their sins to the limit. The wrath of God has come upon them at last.*

Key Observation. God never abandons his people; he is committed to justice.

Understanding the Word. Ever feel abandoned by God? Evil people appear to triumph. Good people suffer. Why doesn't God do something? Where is God when it matters? Those are fair questions. And they're the sort of questions Paul's readers likely asked given the suffering they endured for their public witness to Jesus. That's why he offers a defense of God's justice.

The defense circles around the word *wrath*. We saw it in chapter 1. Now we see it again. We observed in chapter 1 that God's wrath is his measured, consistent, just opposition to anything that antagonizes his good purposes in the world. That's exactly what Paul and the Thessalonians experienced. They were committed to God's mission to fill the world with his beauty, but they faced opposition. Paul compares their struggle with the struggle of the church in Judea. He seems to have in mind a group of Jews (certainly not all Jewish people!) who have opposed God's work from the start. He charges them for being involved in the death of Jesus and for antagonizing the mission of the gospel for the nations. That is, they rejected God's anointed king, and they tried to stop the spread of God's kingdom. Paul insists that God isn't sitting idle while these folks attack his people and undercut the mission.

These verses introduce a new angle on divine wrath. In the previous chapter, Paul spoke of God's wrath as a future reality. Here he describes a present dimension. What does he have in mind? To some extent, all of us have experienced the negative consequences of sin. Hopefully, however, we've repented and turned from that. When Paul speaks of "heap[ing] up their sins to the limit" (v. 16 NIV), he may be suggesting that these opponents are unrelentingly unrepentant. They have given themselves completely to sin. In Romans 1:24–28, Paul speaks of God giving people over to their sin. The idea is that if people repeatedly choose sin, there comes a point when God gives them just what they want. The consequences are deep and abiding. This is likely what Paul means when he speaks of divine wrath in the present. They aren't simply resisting God; God is actively giving them over to their resistance. This is an expression of his judgment against them.

As challenging as that is, Paul aims to comfort the Thessalonians. He's reminding them that God will make things right. God isn't turning a blind eye to the suffering they face. He has not abandoned them, and he has not abandoned you. His work and purposes may not always be easy to understand—but he has not abandoned you. He never will.

1. What does God's commitment to justice say about his character? How does that divine commitment to justice impact your commitment to God?

2. Is there an area of your life in which you are experiencing the consequences of resisting God? Have you repented?

3. Are there injustices in your community that need to be revealed or opposed? What are they? How can you help?

FIVE

Fruit Matters

1 Thessalonians 2:17–20 NIV *But, brothers and sisters, when we were orphaned by being separated from you for a short time (in person, not in thought), out of our intense longing we made every effort to see you. [18]For we wanted to come to you—certainly I, Paul, did, again and again—but Satan blocked our way. [19]For what is our hope, our joy, or the crown in which we will glory in the presence of our Lord Jesus when he comes? Is it not you? [20]Indeed, you are our glory and joy.*

Key Observation. The fruit we cultivate for the kingdom will be revealed when Jesus returns.

Understanding the Word. You don't have to hang out in church very long to discover that some people are unconcerned with fruitfulness. They rarely invite people, and they never tell others the good news about Jesus. They show up with some regularity, but they seem to like things the way they are. Sadly, mission matters little to them.

From Paul's point of view, you don't want to be that kind of person. Fruit matters to Paul. It matters a lot. And it matters to Jesus. These verses may seem strange to those of us who are used to singing: "Nothing in my hands I bring; simply to thy cross I cling."[2] After all, it sounds like Paul plans to boast about his own work. Well, he certainly portrays his fruit among the Thessalonians to have real significance before Jesus when he returns. And that's something

---

2. Thomas Hastings, "Rock of Ages," 1776. Public domain.

we need to take seriously. Their faith gives him reason to boast. They are his hope, his glory, his joy. Is Paul suggesting that he deserves something from God because of the work he's done to plant churches? Does he think he'll be saved because of his effort?

We've found repeatedly that Paul sees the Word of God as the power that sustains believers and produces fruit. So, he's not trying to take credit for God's power; his boasting is not a matter of self-focused pride. What he's expressing is something like the grateful pride a parent feels when they see their children grow up to maturity. When kids grow into healthy adults, it's not evidence that the parents were perfect, but it is evidence that the parents did their job. The continued faithfulness of the Thessalonians shows that Paul has been a faithful instrument through whom God has been at work. And on the day of Christ's return, that will be revealed for all to see. Paul's believing allegiance to Jesus and his mission will be vindicated. The fruit that comes from the Thessalonians will show that Paul didn't waste his life. Their unwavering commitment will crown Paul's head on that day.

This invites us to consider how we're spending our energy. Are we working to help others encounter Jesus for the first time? Are we giving ourselves to helping them become mature believers? Are we committed to serving the mission of the church? Are we committed to making Jesus known? Are we bearing fruit? Or are we in maintenance mode? Do we just show up on occasion so that people won't think bad of us? Or perhaps so we can feel good about ourselves? We do well to remember fruit matters. And the fruit we have (or haven't) cultivated will be revealed in the end.

1. When was the last time you sacrificed to help another person cultivate their relationship with Jesus?

2. What are you actively doing to produce fruit for the kingdom of God?

WEEK TWO

GATHERING DISCUSSION OUTLINE

A. **Open session in prayer.** Ask that God would astonish us anew with fresh insight from God's Word and transform us into the disciples that Jesus desires us to become.

B. **View video for this week's readings.**

C. **What were key insights or takeaways that you gained from your reading during the week and from watching the video commentary?** In particular, how did these help you to grow in your faith and understanding of Scripture this week? What parts of the Bible lessons or study raised questions for you?

D. **Discuss questions selected from the daily readings.** Invite class members to share key insights or to raise questions that they found to be the most meaningful.

1. **KEY OBSERVATION:** All of life should be lived to please God alone.

   DISCUSSION QUESTION: What areas in your life are lived to please someone other than God?

2. **KEY OBSERVATION:** Christian community should be characterized by self-giving love, even in difficult circumstances.

   DISCUSSION QUESTION: What are two or three specific things you can do to cultivate self-giving love in your community?

3. **KEY OBSERVATION:** Faith is trusting God to do what we cannot do for ourselves.

   DISCUSSION QUESTION: How can you begin to trust God more in those areas of life in which you are self-reliant?

4. **KEY OBSERVATION:** God never abandons his people; he is committed to justice.

   DISCUSSION QUESTION: Are there injustices in your community that need to be revealed or opposed? What are they? How can you help?

5. **KEY OBSERVATION:** The fruit we cultivate for the kingdom will be revealed when Jesus returns.

   DISCUSSION QUESTION: What are you actively doing to produce fruit for the kingdom of God?

E. **As the study concludes, consider specific ways that this week's Bible lessons invite you to grow and call you to change.** How do this week's scriptures call us to think differently? How do they challenge us to change in order to align ourselves with God's work in the world? What specific actions should we take to apply the insights of the lessons into our daily lives? What kind of person do our Bible lessons call us to become?

F. **Close session with prayer.** Emphasize God's ongoing work of transformation in our lives in preparation for loving mission and service in the world. Pray for absent class members as well as for persons whom we need to invite to join our study.

WEEK THREE

1 Thessalonians 3:1–13

Keeping Faith, Standing Firm

ONE

Destined for Trouble

1 Thessalonians 3:1–3 *Therefore when we could bear it no longer, we decided to be left alone in Athens;* *²and we sent Timothy, our brother and co-worker for God in proclaiming the gospel of Christ, to strengthen and encourage you for the sake of your faith,* *³so that no one would be shaken by these persecutions. Indeed, you yourselves know that this is what we are destined for.*

Key Observation. The gospel of Jesus often provokes opposition.

Understanding the Word. You can feel the heaviness in his voice. They are his children, but he hasn't heard from them. Could his greatest fear have been realized? Have they fallen? Or are they keeping the faith and standing firm? He must find out. Someone must go.

These are undoubtedly the kind of thoughts Paul had while in Athens. So, he sent Timothy to find out about the Thessalonians. This explains part of Paul's reason for writing. Timothy brought back a good report. The Thessalonians were indeed standing firm. Grateful for the news, Paul writes now to express his joy and address a few questions most likely asked by Timothy on the Thessalonians' behalf. Those topics will occupy chapters 4 and 5. For now, these verses teach us a few things about Paul's attitude toward his mission and ours.

Look at the end of verse 3. Paul claims that he and his hearers were "destined" for persecution. Now we've talked a lot about persecution, but this provides more insight. For Paul, persecution isn't something that might come along when the gospel is proclaimed. Instead, it's a guarantee. Why is that?

First, the gospel declares the universal lordship of Jesus Christ. Often, when we think about Jesus as Lord, we think of him as *our* personal Lord who has authority in *our* individual lives. But the authority of Jesus is not limited to believers, and it's not limited to us as individuals. The gospel claims that Jesus is Lord over everyone and everything. Kings. Presidents. Prime ministers. Principals. Executives. Nations. Like it or not, their authority doesn't belong to them without respect to Jesus. They will either submit to the lordship of Jesus and use their delegated authority in a way that pleases him, or they will resist his authority and insist on being lords to themselves. You don't have to imagine how the power players in the first century took the news of Jesus' universal kingship. Acts 17:7 reports that, while in Thessalonica, Paul was accused of disobeying the emperor for allegedly "saying that there is another king named Jesus." The gospel threatened the king's power.

Second, and on a more personal level, people don't always appreciate the call to confess their sin and repent. Paul remarked earlier how the Thessalonian believers turned from idol worship. How do you think their neighbors felt when Christians stopped honoring Zeus? That's the sort of thing that could get you in big trouble in the ancient Roman Empire. And it illustrates why Paul expected the gospel to illicit opposition.

1. Have you ever been treated poorly while sharing the good news about Jesus? If not, are you willing to suffer mistreatment for the gospel?
   I haven't, but felt like I would be cristicized
2. Do we normally expect our governing authorities to honor King Jesus? Why or why not?
   We hope that they do

TWO

Faith under Attack

1 Thessalonians 3:4–5 *In fact, when we were with you, we told you beforehand that we were to suffer persecution; so it turned out, as you know. ⁵For this reason, when I could bear it no longer, I sent to find out about your faith; I was afraid that somehow the tempter had tempted you and that our labor had been in vain.*

24

Key Observation. Temptation presents the real possibility that followers of Jesus might fall away.

Understanding the Word. We've talked about Paul's fear. Let's turn to the reason for it. In short, he's sees a real possibility that the Thessalonians might succumb to temptation and abandon their faith in Jesus. He worries that they will stop following Jesus and return to idol worship—the Roman Empire status quo.

The whole thing turns on Paul's knowledge of the experience of temptation. He knows the Thessalonians are feeling the pressure. That pressure likely came in different forms. It could've been the threat of physical violence like Paul endured when he was beaten and jailed. It might have been financial pressure generated by those who refused to do business with followers of Jesus. It could've been the subtle suggestion from close friends or family that Jesus didn't deserve their loyalty, especially given the hardship they were enduring. Any of these scenarios might present the temptation to abandon the mission of God.

Behind all these possibilities Paul sees the work of someone he calls "the tempter." He's thinking of Satan, who Paul said kept him from visiting the Thessalonians (2:18). By mentioning Satan's role in tempting the Thessalonians to abandon the mission, Paul reminds them that their sufferings are not isolated incidents. They form part of a larger cosmic battle in which the forces of evil attempt to thwart the mission of God.

Don't get the wrong idea. While Satan and demonic powers oppose God's people, they don't have the power to make people fall away. That only happens when believers forsake the faith. Satan isn't infinite in power. He's not the equal and opposite of Jesus. He's a creature, not a god. If believers resist temptation and keep their eyes on Jesus, they'll be safe.

One more very important observation may have already occurred to you. This is one of the several places where it becomes clear that Paul didn't believe in the notion of once saved, always saved. He considered it a real possibility that the Thessalonians might fall. He didn't think that falling away meant they weren't really Christians. After all, he's affirmed their faith and the power of God working among them. It also doesn't mean that they lose their salvation every time they sin. Jesus is patient and wants to help us overcome sin; he doesn't abandon us when we struggle. But Paul is talking about the possibility that they might walk away from Jesus *entirely*. His point is that believers must persevere in faith. That doesn't mean we're responsible for our salvation. It does mean that we must continue to trust God and offer our allegiance to him in an ongoing fashion. And it reinforces the point that faith is not an interior reality with no outward behavioral implications. The Thessalonians can't say they love Jesus and then live like everyone else. Faith in Jesus means public faithfulness to Jesus.

1. How does it make you feel knowing that your temptations are part of a cosmic battle between good and evil? Will you approach temptation differently now? How?

2. What strategies do you use to resist temptation when it arises?

Prayer

Don't put yourself THREE the situation

Grace in Community

1 Thessalonians 3:6–8 *But Timothy has just now come to us from you, and has brought us the good news of your faith and love. He has told us also that you always remember us kindly and long to see us—just as we long to see you. ⁷For this reason, brothers and sisters, during all our distress and persecution we have been encouraged about you through your faith. ⁸For we now live, if you continue to stand firm in the Lord.*

Key Observation. God works to strengthen believers through Christian community.

Understanding the Word. Imagine Paul's relief. After all his anxiety, all his worry, all his fear, he now knows the Thessalonians are persevering in faith. His work has not been wasted. They remain faithful, and they share his deep desire for reunion.

You may have noticed that Paul is not only thankful for the good news about their faith, he's also glad to hear about their love. Christian faith is always expressed in love. And the Thessalonians are living that pattern. They have shown their love for God because they haven't yielded to persecution. They've demonstrated love for Paul by remaining faithful to what he taught them and cultivating their affection for him. And they've shown love to one another by resisting the temptation to turn on each other as their suffering intensified. If they said they loved Jesus but didn't act accordingly, they would show themselves hypocrites. It was no small thing for Jewish and Gentile believers to forge a new community marked by belief in a crucified and risen Lord, and to defend that community against opposition. For Paul, this is evidence that God is at work.

You get a glimpse here of the value of Christian community. You've got Paul (and his team) and the Thessalonians. They are separated by distance, but the shared knowledge of their mutual love and concern for one another is life-giving to Paul. They need each other. The community strengthens each individual for continued faithfulness. Following Jesus would be so much more difficult—perhaps impossible—without the support and encouragement of sisters and brothers in Christ.

Paul's gratitude for the Thessalonians invites us to consider our own commitment to Christian community. Are we building deep and abiding relationships with other followers of Jesus? Do we meet together regularly not only to worship but to care for one another's souls? Do we attend to each other's needs, both spiritual and physical? Do we notice when fellow believers struggle with temptation? Do we provide loving accountability? Do we help each other stay faithful? These questions point to the value and necessity of serious and committed Christian community.

You may want to consider how you use your time in an average week. How do you cultivate deep community with other Christ-followers? Compare that to the time you give to recreation, entertainment, work, and other things. If you lack vitality in your Christian life, it may well be related to the amount of time you give (or don't give) to deepening relationships with other believers.

Paul also knows that the battle isn't over; he understands the need for continued faithfulness and perseverance. He's received a good report, he's encouraged, he can even take a sigh of relief—but more work remains to be done. The Thessalonians must be vigilant and "continue to stand firm in the Lord." And as the letter continues, he'll have some things to say about how they do that.

1. Describe your experience of Christian community. Is it shallow or deep? Why?

Church Bible Study Wed nights Christian music Try to align w/ like minded people

2. What needs to change in your life in order to make Christian community a higher priority? *Daily devotion*

3. How does Christian community relate to the mission of God to rescue the nations?

FOUR

Complete Transformation

1 Thessalonians 3:9–10 *How can we thank God enough for you in return for all the joy that we feel before our God because of you?* [10]*Night and day we pray most earnestly that we may see you face to face and restore whatever is lacking in your faith.*

Key Observation. Mature disciples see everything through the lens of the gospel.

Understanding the Word. The last six words in verse 10 may surprise you. Timothy had brought back a good report. The Thessalonians were standing firm in the face of persecution. Paul has expressed deep joy over their perseverance. What could possibly be lacking?

Remember that Paul sees the Thessalonians as his children. They became followers of Jesus through his ministry, and they are progressing well. But they are still young in faith. And he wants to be sure they grow to full maturity. It may help to remember that, for Paul, faith is not simply an intellectual commitment to a principle or idea. Throughout the letter we've seen how he expects followers of Jesus to live out the implications of their faith. When he writes about what is lacking in their faith, he's not talking about their first experience of believing the gospel, as if they need to believe *more* or believe *harder* to be sure they are saved. He's talking about how that faith relates to the range of experiences and situations they face. They need to learn to apply the gospel more broadly to every area of life. Their faith needs to grow into mature faithfulness.

What does that involve? It involves seeing everything through the lens of the gospel. If the crucified and risen Jesus is Lord, what does it mean for my marriage? Does the love between me and my spouse embody the self-giving

28

love of Christ revealed on the cross (cf. Ephesians 5:25–27)? What about our kids? What does gospel-oriented parenting look like? Do we understand that our primary responsibility to our children is to cultivate in them the character of Christ? And how does the gospel apply to our friendships? Our work relationships? Do we consider the gospel when we make choices about entertainment? Does the truth of the gospel govern our calendar, or do we allow other concerns to determine our schedules? The way we spend our time says a lot about what we love most.

What we're talking about is the transformation of our whole lives. Paul knows that the Lord Jesus Christ isn't satisfied with only our initial profession of faith. That is certainly important; in fact, it's crucial. But we must understand that conversion is the first step, not the goal. Christian discipleship is a long-term project. It will likely take time to learn how to see all of life through the lens of the gospel. And certain opportunities for growth only come in certain seasons of life. Adolescent believers are likely learning different lessons than middle-aged believers. Paul wanted the Thessalonians to develop a mature faith that habitually applies the gospel to everything. That's the goal for us too.

1. Think of the spheres of your life: relationships, work, finances, health, hobbies, spirituality. How do you live out the gospel in each of these areas of life? Which areas are lived in light of the gospel? Which are not?

2. What can you do to daily cultivate an increasing gospel-focus?

Daily devotion

FIVE

Grace for Holy Love

1 Thessalonians 3:11–13 *Now may our God and Father himself and our Lord Jesus direct our way to you. ¹²And may the Lord make you increase and abound in love for one another and for all, just as we abound in love for you. ¹³And may he so strengthen your hearts in holiness that you may be blameless before our God and Father at the coming of our Lord Jesus with all his saints.*

Key Observation. God enables believers to embody holy love.

Understanding the Word. Everything Paul has said is driving toward this point. His call for Christlike perseverance and total transformation together implied what is now explicit. There is one word that describes what Paul wants for his readers—*holiness*. The word *holiness* is often misunderstood. For some, it suggests a legalistic adherence to a list of rules. For others, it entails an unrealistic standard of behavior. But in these verses Paul's talk of holiness sits alongside talk of overabounding love. And he seems to think it's possible. What do we make of that?

First, note that these verses are written as a prayer and they come at the end of the first major section of the letter. First Thessalonians 1:1–3:13 describes Paul's concern about the recipients, while 1 Thessalonians 4:1–5:28 will focus on specific issues to be resolved. There's a similar prayer for holiness that comes at the end of that second major section (5:23–24). That means everything Paul says in both sections comes to its pastoral climax in prayer that God will make the Thessalonians holy. The call to holiness binds everything in this letter together.

So, how should we think about holiness? These verses make two points. First, Paul understands holiness in terms of love. Look at the parallel structure in verses 12 and 13: "may the Lord make you . . . abound in love . . . may he . . . strengthen your hearts in holiness." In two consecutive verses Jesus is said to increase love and holiness. That means the two should be understood in light of each other. Now we need to be careful here, because the word *love* is used in a variety of ways in our culture. What specifically does Paul mean? Some people use the word *love* to describe affection or emotional attachment. Others use it to demand uncritical acceptance of their own behavior. But that's not what Paul is thinking. He offers specific ways to correct behaviors precisely because he loves the Thessalonians. For Paul, *holy love* is the self-giving love of Jesus embodied in his death on the cross. Jesus suffered infinite pain to rescue us from sin. That's love. Paul exemplifies that love in his relationship with the Thessalonians, and he wants that same holy love to characterize their relationships.

Second, growth in holiness happens by grace through faith. God enables us to grow in holy love. It's not done simply by mustering our strength. But that doesn't mean we're entirely passive. We receive the grace that makes us holy, trusting God can change us. That trust is expressed through faithful surrender to God's transforming power. Know that if that happens, it's only because of God's powerful work in us. But he doesn't change us against our will. We must cooperate. If we want to embody God's holy love, we must obey.

1. What was your understanding of holiness before today's lesson? Does it change your understanding of holiness to think of it in terms of self-giving love? ?

2. Are you cooperating with God or resisting him? a little of both

3. How can group members help each other grow in holy love?

Consistent prayer
loving
Equiping
laboring
Witnessing

Who helped you in your faith?
If they saw you today, would they be happy?
Who have you helped grow in their faith?

WEEK THREE

GATHERING DISCUSSION OUTLINE

A. **Open session in prayer.** Ask that God would astonish us anew with fresh insight from God's Word and transform us into the disciples that Jesus desires us to become.

B. **View video for this week's readings.**

C. **What were key insights or takeaways that you gained from your reading during the week and from watching the video commentary?** In particular, how did these help you to grow in your faith and understanding of Scripture this week? What parts of the Bible lessons or study raised questions for you?

D. **Discuss questions selected from the daily readings.** Invite class members to share key insights or to raise questions that they found to be the most meaningful.

1. **KEY OBSERVATION:** The gospel of Jesus often provokes opposition.

   DISCUSSION QUESTION: Have you ever been treated poorly while sharing the good news about Jesus? If not, are you willing to suffer mistreatment for the gospel?

2. **KEY OBSERVATION:** Temptation presents the real possibility that followers of Jesus might fall away.

   DISCUSSION QUESTION: What strategies do you use to resist temptation when it arises?

3. **KEY OBSERVATION:** God works to strengthen believers through Christian community.

   DISCUSSION QUESTION: How does Christian community relate to the mission of God to rescue the nations?

4. **KEY OBSERVATION:** Mature disciples see everything through the lens of the gospel.

   DISCUSSION QUESTION: What can you do to daily cultivate an increasing gospel-focus?

5. **KEY OBSERVATION:** God enables believers to embody holy love.

   DISCUSSION QUESTION: How can group members help each other grow in holy love?

E. **As the study concludes, consider specific ways that this week's Bible lessons invite you to grow and call you to change.** How do this week's scriptures call us to think differently? How do they challenge us to change in order to align ourselves with God's work in the world? What specific actions should we take to apply the insights of the lessons into our daily lives? What kind of person do our Bible lessons call us to become?

F. **Close session with prayer.** Emphasize God's ongoing work of transformation in our lives in preparation for loving mission and service in the world. Pray for absent class members as well as for persons whom we need to invite to join our study.

1 Thessalonians 4:1–18

Holy Bodies, New Bodies

ONE

Start with Holy

1 Thessalonians 4:1–3a NIV *As for other matters, brothers and sisters, we instructed you how to live in order to please God, as in fact you are living. Now we ask you and urge you in the Lord Jesus to do this more and more. ²For you know what instructions we gave you by the authority of the Lord Jesus.*

³It is God's will that you should be sanctified . . .

Key Observation. Holiness is God's will for your life.

Understanding the Word. Most of us want to know God's plan. We want direction. We want purpose. *What's God's will for me?* If you've asked that question, you may be surprised to discover God's will is the same for everyone. And it's summed up with one word—*sanctification*. Sanctification refers to the process of becoming holy. For Paul, everything else is secondary. If you want to know God's will for your life, start with holy.

If you're wondering why Paul thinks this way, consider that he grew up immersed in the Old Testament. One passage that fills in the picture is found in Ezekiel 36, which anticipates the day God will rescue his people from exile. How did they get to the point of exile? They had given themselves to sin for so long that God had to do something drastic to get their attention: he allowed foreign powers to conquer them and take them out of their land (vv. 18–19). We've already learned from Paul that God never gives up on his people, and that's Ezekiel's message too. Ezekiel promised the Hebrew people that God would rescue them. But the plan was not simply to rescue them from foreign captivity; God intended to rescue them from their sin—*all of it*. After all, sin was the root problem. To do that, God would have to change them from the inside out, give them new hearts. He even promised to give his own Holy Spirit to empower obedience. God will make his people holy. And here's the reason: "the nations shall know that I am the LORD . . . when through you I display my holiness before their eyes" (Ezek. 36:23). Catch that? God's plan is to show the nations the beauty of his holiness, and the bodies of his people will be the theater where that holiness is enacted.

That means that God must deal with our sin. He must show us the ways our lives aren't aligned with his character. If we surrender to that work, we get the remarkable privilege of showing God's holy love to the world. God is faithful. He always does what's right. He always tells the truth. There's no duplicity in him. No deceit. He wants those aspects of his character to consistently define the lives of his people. And that's how God intends to make his character known to every nation on earth, which means holiness is ultimately about mission.

Do you want people to know God's holy love? Because he wants to show his holy love to other people *through you*. Think about that. The world will know God is God when his people embody his holy character. That's his will for all of us. Everything else is secondary.

1. Think of a time you had a big decision to make. What did you do? Would you have decided differently by prioritizing holiness as God's plan for you?

2. God wants his people to show the nations his holiness. How are holiness and mission intertwined in this passage?

3. Why is our personal holiness critical for God's witness in the world?

Pray about every decision

TWO

Holiness Happens in Community

1 Thessalonians 4:3–8 NIV *It is God's will that you should be sanctified: that you should avoid sexual immorality; ⁴that each of you should learn to control* *your own body in a way that is holy and honorable, ⁵not in passionate lust like the pagans, who do not know God; ⁶and that in this matter no one should wrong or take advantage of a brother or sister. The Lord will punish all those who commit such sins, as we told you and warned you before. ⁷For God did not call us to be impure, but to live a holy life. ⁸Therefore, anyone who rejects this instruction does not reject a human being but God, the very God who gives you his Holy Spirit.*

Key Observation. Growth in holiness requires deep commitment to Christian community.

Understanding the Word. John Wesley's commitment to proclaiming holiness changed the world. If you've never heard of Wesley, he started the Methodist movement that now spans the globe. He famously said, "'Holy solitaries' is a phrase no more consistent with the gospel than holy adulterers. The gospel of Christ knows . . . no holiness but social holiness."[3] The language is somewhat antiquated, but the point remains. Holiness is not a solo gig. Growth in Christian maturity isn't something we can do alone. It takes a social group, a community of people looking after one another in love. Wesley understood this reality because he saw that scriptural teaching on holiness presupposes the community of believers. This is particularly important in our day because a growing number of people see Christian faith in individualistic terms. They think following Jesus carries no expectations for commitment to a local church. As a pastor, I meet people all the time who insist they are saved even though they haven't participated in any Christian community for a very, very long time. This is a strange idea, not only to Wesley, but also to Paul.

This passage in 1 Thessalonians illustrates the point. Paul moves directly from talk of holiness to instructions on how believers treat each other. If they are going to be holy, it means they must behave toward one another in very specific ways. Holiness is forged in relationships. We all know what it's like to have our patience tested by the people around us. We've been tempted to speak harshly to people we love. Holiness means embodying the character of God toward others when we are tempted to treat them with contempt.

---

3. John Wesley, *The Works of John Wesley,* ed. Thomas Jackson (Grand Rapids: Baker, 1872, 2007), XIV: 321.

Now this can be applied in any number of ways. But in this passage, Paul found it necessary to deal with the sensitive topic of sex. He expects the Thessalonians to "avoid sexual immorality." The Greek word translated as "sexual immorality" is *porneia*, a catch-all term for nearly every form of sexual behavior other than sex between a husband and wife. It was common in Roman cities like Thessalonica for men to see sex as a matter of competition, conquest, and grounds for boasting. Paul rejects this fundamentally self-oriented practice and insists that believers control themselves and treat each other respectfully and with honor.

Paul expected the Christian community in Thessalonica to be different. The group is defined by their holy behavior in contrast to those around them. Pay attention to how important the community is. If you're going to turn from a posture of self-orientation to other-oriented love, it takes the presence of others. And the holy character of that group distinguishes it from other groups. Holiness happens in community.

1. How deeply are you embedded in Christian community? Are there other believers who help you grow in holiness? What does that look like?

2. Can you think of a time of significant growth as a Christian? What role did Christian community play in that? Would facing that situation alone have led to a different outcome?

THREE

Holiness Means Abounding Love

1 Thessalonians 4:9–12 NIV *Now about your love for one another we do not need to write to you, for you yourselves have been taught by God to love each other. ¹⁰And in fact, you do love all of God's family throughout Macedonia. Yet we urge you, brothers and sisters, to do so more and more, ¹¹and to make it your ambition to lead a quiet life: You should mind your own business and work with your hands, just as we told you, ¹²so that your daily life may win the respect of outsiders and so that you will not be dependent on anybody.*

Key Observation. Holiness is overflowing love, not legalistic rule-following.

Understanding the Word. A lot of people are intimidated by the language of holiness. After all, it seems impossible. We know ourselves too well; we know our brokenness and the secret darkness in our hearts. How could we keep all the rules? How can we possibly be holy? Well, if we think of holiness like that—focused on checking a list of behaviors—we are destined to fail. Fortunately, holiness isn't a legalistic obsession with the rules. It's a heart that overflows with love.

That's how Paul understands holiness. And that's what he wants the Thessalonians to do. That's also why he follows his insistence on holiness with talk of abounding love. He acknowledges that the Thessalonians love each other. That's good. But the thing about love is that you can't have too much. Paul continues by telling the recipients to love one another "more and more." And here's the thing: if your heart is overflowing with love, you won't be sinning against the people around you. You can't love and sin at the same time.

Think about it in light of what we've already learned this week. Paul expects the Thessalonians to be holy. This means they can't use one another for their own sexual gratification. They can't exploit each other. Exploitation isn't love; it's sin. If they abound in love, they won't see people as objects to be used, not least with regard to sex. Instead, they'll treat each other with dignity, respect, and honor. They'll embody the character of Jesus to one another. They'll be holy.

Thinking about holiness exclusively in terms of a list of things we should and shouldn't do takes our focus away from love and puts it on performance. Of course, if we are treating other people with love, there are things we will do and things we won't. But the focus is on loving the other person, not performing for them. Holy love means we behave in certain ways. But the behavior flows from a heart filled with love, not the other way around.

It may be helpful to recall that Jesus summarized the whole law with two commandments: "'You shall love the Lord your God with all your heart, and with all your soul, and with all your mind.' . . . And . . . 'You shall love your neighbor as yourself'" (Matt. 22:37–39). For Jesus, the law of God is about teaching people to love. This means our fundamental orientation is not toward ourselves but toward God and neighbor. That's why love and sin stand in fundamental opposition. Sin happens when I am oriented toward myself—doing life on my terms. Holiness is the fruit of a life oriented toward God and surrendered fully to God. When that happens, God's holy love is expressed through us toward the people around us.

1. What do you think of when you hear the word *holy*? Rules to be obeyed? A performance to be maintained? How does the term *holy love* challenge and transform your understanding of holiness?

2. Do you think a person's life can be consistently marked by holy love? Why or why not?

FOUR

Christian Hope Is Resurrection Hope

1 Thessalonians 4:13–18 NIV *Brothers and sisters, we do not want you to be uninformed about those who sleep in death, so that you do not grieve like the rest of mankind, who have no hope.* [14]*For we believe that Jesus died and rose again, and so we believe that God will bring with Jesus those who have fallen asleep in him.* [15]*According to the Lord's word, we tell you that we who are still alive, who are left until the coming of the Lord, will certainly not precede those who have fallen asleep.* [16]*For the Lord himself will come down from heaven, with a loud command, with the voice of the archangel and with the trumpet call of God, and the dead in Christ will rise first.* [17]*After that, we who are still alive and are left will be caught up together with them in the clouds to meet the Lord in the air. And so we will be with the Lord forever.* [18]*Therefore encourage one another with these words.*

Key Observation. Christian hope is hope for bodily resurrection.

Understanding the Word. The most common set of questions I'm asked as a pastor have to do with life after death. People want to know what happens when this life ends. Paul appears to have received questions like that too. And he's eager to explain. He doesn't want his recipients to be misinformed about Christian hope.

For Paul, hope is all about the resurrection of the body. Why? Because that's what happened to Jesus after he died. And Paul sees Jesus as the prototype for Christian hope. Jesus died. Then his body was raised from the dead. The same body that went into the tomb on the first Good Friday came out of the tomb on the first Easter Sunday. His physical body was raised still marked by the scars of crucifixion. But it was different too; his body had been transformed. It was no longer mortal. Try to imagine a human body that can't die or break or get sick, and you'll be well on your way to imagining what Jesus' resurrection body is like.

If Jesus died and was raised bodily from the dead, then that is what his people should expect also. That's what we hope for—bodily resurrection. And Paul says that's exactly what will happen. And he expects it to happen when Jesus returns. That return will be a public celebration, with angels shouting and trumpets playing. And when Jesus comes, he will bring those who have died, and he will raise them from the dead. Right now, they are consciously present with Jesus in heaven, but that is not their final hope. People in heaven are still waiting for the climax of their salvation. That will happen when their bodies are transformed and glorified—just like Jesus.

When I'm preaching on resurrection, I often remark that I hope to be walking near my dad's grave when Jesus comes back. I long to be in that place and see the sod break and the vault crack and the hinges on the casket come loose as the power of the grave is finally broken and my dad is raised bodily from the dead. I hope we get to see Jesus return together.

That is Paul's point to the grieving Thessalonians. They want to know their loved ones are safe. Paul assures them that they are and, not only that, but that they will be reunited in the presence of Christ as well. Hope for resurrection says that, for those who belong to Christ, you will see your loved ones again. You will feel their embrace. You will see their smile. You will hear their voice. And all in the presence of Jesus. That's hope. That's real hope. That's our hope.

1. What was your understanding of Christian hope before reading this passage? Does Paul's teaching on our resurrection hope challenge or change your understanding of hope?

2. Try to imagine your body free from the effects of sin and death. What would that be like? What sorts of things might you do? How does that relate to your understanding of heaven?

3. Do you think hope for bodily resurrection is widespread among Christians? Why or why not?

1 Corinthians 15

FIVE

Grief Wrapped in Hope

1 Thessalonians 4:13–18 NIV *Brothers and sisters, we do not want you to be uninformed about those who sleep in death, so that you do not grieve like the rest of mankind, who have no hope. ¹⁴For we believe that Jesus died and rose again, and so we believe that God will bring with Jesus those who have fallen asleep in him. ¹⁵According to the Lord's word, we tell you that we who are still alive, who are left until the coming of the Lord, will certainly not precede those who have fallen asleep. ¹⁶For the Lord himself will come down from heaven, with a loud command, with the voice of the archangel and with the trumpet call of God, and the dead in Christ will rise first. ¹⁷After that, we who are still alive and are left will be caught up together with them in the clouds to meet the Lord in the air. And so we will be with the Lord forever. ¹⁸Therefore encourage one another with these words.*

Key Observation. Future bodily resurrection transforms grief from despair to hope.

Understanding the Word. Many people are crippled by grief. It's that sick feeling deep in the gut when someone we love is taken from us and there's nothing we can do about it. It isn't fair. We have no control. We just hurt. Death feels so final. Paul understands that and he acknowledges the deep reality of grief as he writes this passage. He contrasts those who grieve *without hope* to those who grieve *in hope*. Either way, people grieve. The question is whether we grieve well. And many do not. You see, the pain of grief is so great that people often feel they can't handle it. So they suppress it; they push their grief away. But it doesn't go away, it just goes into hiding. And it always comes out, often when we least expect it.

Paul is giving the Thessalonians (and us) permission to grieve. Sometimes that's all we need. We need to know it's okay to acknowledge the pain we feel in the face of death. We need to be honest about how hurt we are. But we also need to remember that the grave does not have the last word. Jesus does. He's the one who has defeated death. He's the one whose body can never die again. And he's the one who will raise the dead when he returns to reign visibly over this world. That transforms grief and fills it with hope. And it should encourage us, because it means our pain is not ultimate. It's temporary. Resurrection is coming.

I always encourage people who are grieving to find healthy ways to acknowledge the reality of their sorrow and to focus on hope. Perhaps you need to do just that. It can be as simple as taking a few minutes to pray and tell God how bad your pain is and to thank him for the hope for resurrection that we have through Jesus. You could plan a gathering with family on the anniversary of a loved one's passing. Take time together to articulate your shared pain. Just be sure you also take time to give glory to the God who raised Jesus from the dead—the God who will raise all of us from the dead. If you engage in these kinds of practices, you'll be doing just what Paul instructed the Thessalonians to do: "encourage one another with these words."

Before we conclude today's lesson, allow me to speak directly to pastors who may read this book. Let me encourage you to always be sure your funeral sermons are focused on the hope for resurrection. I've been to far too many funerals where resurrection received little or no attention. They focus instead on the soul's escape to a disembodied heaven. The trouble is that dying and going to heaven reinforces the fact that the body is still dead. The grave remains the victor. Death has not yet been defeated. Christian hope is not hope for a disembodied afterlife; it's hope for physical resurrection. And the funeral sermon is a key moment for pastors to articulate our hope for resurrection. Every funeral in which I've preached a robust theology of resurrection has been met with gratitude from those who heard. I'm confident the same will be the case for you. Whatever you do, preach resurrection hope.

1. Take a moment to think about someone whose death you grieve. Are you grieving that person's death in a healthy way or in an unhealthy way? What are some concrete steps you can take to move toward healthy grief?

2. Think about the last funeral you attended. Did the preacher talk about resurrection? If so, how did that affect you? If not, how might the funeral have been different had the preacher spoken of resurrection?

WEEK FOUR

GATHERING DISCUSSION OUTLINE

A. **Open session in prayer.** Ask that God would astonish us anew with fresh insight from God's Word and transform us into the disciples that Jesus desires us to become.

B. **View video for this week's readings.**

C. **What were key insights or takeaways that you gained from your reading during the week and from watching the video commentary?** In particular, how did these help you to grow in your faith and understanding of Scripture this week? What parts of the Bible lessons or study raised questions for you?

D. **Discuss questions selected from the daily readings.** Invite class members to share key insights or to raise questions that they found to be the most meaningful.

1. **KEY OBSERVATION:** Holiness is God's will for your life.

   DISCUSSION QUESTION: Why is our personal holiness critical for God's witness in the world?

2. **KEY OBSERVATION:** Growth in holiness requires deep commitment to Christian community.

   DISCUSSION QUESTION: How deeply are you embedded in Christian community? Are there other believers who help you grow in holiness? What does that look like?

3. **KEY OBSERVATION:** Holiness is overflowing love, not legalistic rule-following.

   DISCUSSION QUESTION: What do you think of when you hear the word *holy*? Rules to be obeyed? A performance to be maintained? How does the term *holy love* challenge and transform your understanding of holiness?

4. **KEY OBSERVATION:** Christian hope is hope for bodily resurrection.

   DISCUSSION QUESTION: Do you think hope for bodily resurrection is widespread among Christians? Why or why not?

5. **KEY OBSERVATION:** Future bodily resurrection transforms grief from despair to hope.

   DISCUSSION QUESTION: Think about the last funeral you attended. Did the preacher talk about resurrection? If so, how did that affect you? If not, how might the funeral have been different had the preacher spoken of resurrection?

E. **As the study concludes, consider specific ways that this week's Bible lessons invite you to grow and call you to change.** How do this week's scriptures call us to think differently? How do they challenge us to change in order to align ourselves with God's work in the world? What specific actions should we take to apply the insights of the lessons into our daily lives? What kind of person do our Bible lessons call us to become?

F. **Close session with prayer.** Emphasize God's ongoing work of transformation in our lives in preparation for loving mission and service in the world. Pray for absent class members as well as for persons whom we need to invite to join our study.

WEEK FIVE

1 Thessalonians 5:1–28

Standing Firm, Becoming Holy

ONE

Don't Predict; Prepare

1 Thessalonians 5:1–3 *Now concerning the times and the seasons, brothers and sisters, you do not need to have anything written to you. ²For you yourselves know very well that the day of the Lord will come like a thief in the night. ³When they say, "There is peace and security," then sudden destruction will come upon them, as labor pains come upon a pregnant woman, and there will be no escape!*

Key Observation. People should prepare for Jesus' return, not predict its timing.

Understanding the Word. Occasionally someone or some group will claim they've determined the date of Jesus' return. The prediction is usually based on coded calculations about signs of the times. In each case, the anticipated day arrived, but Jesus didn't. You'd think such self-styled prophets would learn to stop making predictions, especially since Scripture doesn't disclose the timing of that all-important event. That's Paul's point here. It's likely he's writing to correct some small-time local prophets who were confusing the Thessalonians with predictions about Jesus' second coming. It's also possible that they simply needed additional instruction about that day. Either way, Paul wants the Thessalonians to be ready for Jesus' return. He doesn't want them predicting the timing of it.

When Paul speaks of "the day of the Lord," he is referring to the return (or second coming) of Jesus to this world. Paul has described his expectations regarding that day in several places in the letter, though he doesn't always use the explicit "day of the Lord" terminology. Let's take a minute to review what he's said so far. Paul says that the recipients are waiting for Jesus—God's Son—to return to earth from heaven (1:10). They are anticipating the day of the Lord, but the timing of that day cannot be predicted. The date is unknown, even though the event is expected. It will come without warning, "like a thief in the night" (5:2). And the experience of that day will vary depending on whether you belong to Jesus or not. Those who belong to Jesus will be raised bodily from the dead (4:16). Paul says elsewhere that believers who are alive at the Lord's coming will also receive resurrection bodies (see 1 Corinthians 15:51–53). For those who don't belong to Jesus, that day will be marked by "wrath" (1 Thess. 1:10) and "destruction" (5:3). Remember that God's wrath is not some sort of unhinged fury. (See commentary on verse 1:10 in Week One, Day Five.) Paul's talk of divine wrath involves God's good, right, and just opposition to all that sets itself against his good creation and his good purposes.

The apostle insists that God's judgment will come against those who set themselves against God. Paul is likely critiquing the Roman Empire here. That was, after all, the reality in which he lived and worked. And "peace and security" is precisely what Rome promised during the first century. Archaeologists have found numerous inscriptions from that period with just that sort of language. But the peace Rome promised was peace on Rome's terms for those who upheld Roman values. The persecution experienced by the Thessalonians (even if it's local and unofficial) makes the point. Disrupt the status quo and you'll find little security. The safety offered by the kingdoms of this world is shown to be a parody when seen in light of the day of the Lord. On that day, the deception will be laid bare before the judgment of King Jesus.

1. Consider the images of a thief and a woman in labor. How do they strengthen the urgent tone of these verses? Why is that urgency important?

2. What are concrete ways you can prepare for Jesus' return?

TWO

Remember Who You Are

1 Thessalonians 5:4–7 *But you, beloved, are not in darkness, for that day to surprise you like a thief; ⁵for you are all children of light and children of the day; we are not of the night or of darkness. ⁶So then let us not fall asleep as others do, but let us keep awake and be sober; ⁷for those who sleep sleep at night, and those who are drunk get drunk at night.*

Key Observation. Christian behavior should reflect Christian identity.

Understanding the Word. "Remember who you are." My grandmother spoke those words to me and my brother as she handed us our jackets. We were heading out the door to meet some friends. I have no idea what she thought we might do. Nevertheless, her point was clear. She wanted us to remember that our family had a good reputation. She didn't want us to damage it. Our grandmother expected our behavior to accord with our family identity.

That's also what Paul expects of the Thessalonians. You can see his logic in the movement from 1 Thessalonians 5:5 to 5:6. He begins by reminding the Thessalonians of their identity. He wants them to remember who they are. And here Christian identity is described in terms of the future. Christians are "children of light and children of the day." To identify believers as light-people was Paul's way of saying they belong to Jesus. For Paul, God has lifted the blinders and led believers out of darkness to "the light of the knowledge of the glory of God in the face of Jesus Christ" (2 Cor. 4:6). Light-people know God because they've seen God in Jesus.

Notice also that Paul uses family language to describe believers. They are *children* of light and of the day. Paul's original Greek actually used a word that means "sons," but translators rightly render it "children" to be inclusive of men and women. The importance of family relationships in the ancient world cannot be overstated. You take your identity from your family, and you owe your loyalty to your family. Paul's use of family language to describe the identity of the group reinforces the deep emotions that would be attached to this new family of God.

Not only are they identified as light-people, they are also day-people. The day in question is the day of the Lord. They belong to Jesus. And the day of his return will be the day that all the implications of their identity in Christ will be revealed. For the Thessalonians, their identification with Jesus makes them a mockery among outsiders. They suffer for it. But on the day of the Lord, they'll be vindicated. They'll participate in his resurrection. Their union with him will come to its fullness. But if they are going to make it, they've got to remember who they are in Christ and who they are together.

1. Take a moment to think about your sense of identity. What are the primary relationships that define your sense of self? Family? Church? School? What needs to change in order for your primary identity to be found in relation to Christ and the community of believers?

2. Think of the last time you struggled with a major life decision. Did your identity as a follower of Jesus and a member of Christian community figure into that decision?

3. In what ways does your sense of self shape your behavior?

THREE

From Distraction to Discipline

1 Thessalonians 5:8–11 *But since we belong to the day, let us be sober, and put on the breastplate of faith and love, and for a helmet the hope of salvation. [9]For God has destined us not for wrath but for obtaining salvation through our Lord Jesus Christ, [10]who died for us, so that whether we are awake or asleep we may live with him. [11]Therefore encourage one another and build up each other, as indeed you are doing.*

Key Observation. Staying faithful and avoiding distraction takes discipline and community.

Understanding the Word. It's easy to get distracted. After all, we are constantly bombarded with voices fighting for our attention and people fighting for our time. Whether it's the lure of social media or responsibilities at work, following Jesus can easily become one thing among many in the busyness of life. Remaining faithful takes discipline and community.

Paul makes his point about the need for discipline by using armor language. Soldiers wear breastplates and helmets, and they must be disciplined for those tools to have their maximum effectiveness. To maintain that discipline, soldiers are always training, always working to get better, to be more effective. They are focused on their mission. They can't allow anything to distract them from their objective.

Paul wants the Thessalonians (and us!) to have that kind of disciplined focus in the way we follow Jesus together. That means two things. First, we must identify potential distractions. What are the things that could potentially draw us away from Jesus? And, remember, the temptations can be subtle. Am I focusing so much on work that I'm not able to be deeply involved in Christian community? Does my recreation (hunting, team sports, etc.) leave too little time to guide my family's devotional life? The most dangerous distractions are seldom the really flagrant sins, though care must be taken to guard against those too. The most dangerous distractions are the ones we think little of—the normal, everyday life stuff—because we give ourselves to those things without really thinking about it. Persevering in faithfulness will take learning to pay attention to the things we easily overlook.

Second, we must cultivate the virtues of faith, hope, and love. It's not enough to only guard against potential dangers; it's also necessary to cultivate positive virtues. The three virtues of faith, love, and hope have appeared repeatedly in 1 Thessalonians. And Paul has largely affirmed the audience's attention to the first two. His extensive teaching on the resurrection (4:13–18) and the day of the Lord (5:1–11) suggest that they need some work in the area of hope. Paul reiterates the point: maximum faithfulness means cultivating all three.

In addition to discipline, it's also important to be grounded in Christian community. This comes through in Paul's exhortation to encourage and build each other up. Faithful perseverance as a follower of Jesus is not a solo gig. Following Jesus was never intended to be something we do alone. We need the family of believers to offer care, support, instruction, and even correction. Without that kind of community, we're more likely to stumble and fall.

1. What activities have the potential to distract you from following Jesus? Pay close attention to the normal activities that may be part of your routine.

2. What disciplines are you cultivating to strengthen yourself spiritually?

FOUR

Community Priority

1 Thessalonians 5:12–22 *But we appeal to you, brothers and sisters, to respect those who labor among you, and have charge of you in the Lord and admonish you; ¹³esteem them very highly in love because of their work. Be at peace among yourselves. ¹⁴And we urge you, beloved, to admonish the idlers, encourage the fainthearted, help the weak, be patient with all of them. ¹⁵See that none of you repays evil for evil, but always seek to do good to one another and to all. ¹⁶Rejoice always, ¹⁷pray without ceasing, ¹⁸give thanks in all circumstances; for this is the will of God in Christ Jesus for you. ¹⁹Do not quench the Spirit. ²⁰Do not despise the words of prophets, ²¹but test everything; hold fast to what is good; ²²abstain from every form of evil.*

Key Observation. Community doesn't happen by accident; it takes hard work.

Understanding the Word. As Paul begins to wrap this letter up, he provides a series of instructions aimed at helping the Thessalonians take the next step down the path of faithfulness. The community of believers is presupposed in many of these commands. That's clear enough because so much of the instruction is focused on how group members relate to one another. Why all this instruction about keeping community? Because community doesn't just happen; it takes a lot of hard work.

Paul starts with a word about leadership. He wants the Thessalonians to love and respect those charged with shepherding the community. It's easy enough to see why he needs to make this point. Leaders must make difficult decisions. And every leader knows you can't make everyone happy all the time. Paul mentions specifically that these leaders are responsible to admonish (or correct) people in their care. You can imagine that some group members may not appreciate such admonishment. But wise and careful leadership is essential for maintaining the community. And Paul wants the Thessalonians to be attentive to that. A community with no leaders is a community with no vision and no direction. It won't be a community for long.

After addressing the issue of leadership, Paul mentions several ways group members can look after each other. If someone isn't carrying his fair share of responsibility, the others should correct that person with love. If another is struggling in some way, the community should offer support and encouragement. They must all be attentive to the needs of the weak. And everyone is responsible for maintaining the peace. The thing to see is that if no one attends to these matters, the community will be rife with conflict and important matters will be left unattended. If they are going to have a healthy community of believers, then they are going to have to work at it. That goes for us too.

Paul also wants their shared life to be marked by the positive presence of God's Holy Spirit. This means they'll be focused on rejoicing, praying, and showing gratitude. They'll be looking for ways to treat each other well. They'll be attentive to the teaching they receive, all the while testing it to ensure its trustworthiness. It's easy to skim over lists like the one Paul offers here. The commands seem so generic and obvious, but we'll do well to pause and reflect on the point that keeps showing up again and again: keeping community takes serious work.

1. Take a moment to think about the value of good leadership in Christian community. What are some concrete things you can do to encourage your leaders and strengthen their ministry for the sake of the whole community?

2. Think of a time you've been tempted to act in a way that undercut someone in your community. What did you do? What was the impact on the community as a whole?

3. How are you actively promoting Christian community?

FIVE

End with Holy

1 Thessalonians 5:23–28 *May the God of peace himself sanctify you entirely; and may your spirit and soul and body be kept sound and blameless at the coming of our Lord Jesus Christ.* ²⁴*The one who calls you is faithful, and he will do this.*

²⁵*Beloved, pray for us.*

²⁶*Greet all the brothers and sisters with a holy kiss.* ²⁷*I solemnly command you by the Lord that this letter be read to all of them.*

²⁸*The grace of our Lord Jesus Christ be with you.*

Key Observation. God's grace can transform us completely.

Understanding the Word. Last words matter. The last thing Paul writes in this letter is what he wants the recipients to hold on to above all else. We shouldn't be surprised that Paul ends his letter with a prayer of blessing in which he calls on God to make the Thessalonians holy. Holiness is a big deal for Paul. You'll remember that in 4:3 he insisted that holiness (sanctification) is God's will for everyone. Now he reminds them of that again. Start with holy and end with holy, and you can be sure that you'll be on track.

The first thing that always strikes me about this prayer is the focus on grace. Sure, the word *grace* doesn't appear until the last sentence, but the concept of grace shows up with the initial insistence that God is the faithful one who makes his people holy. Holiness is not something that can be achieved merely by working harder. No, that's a recipe for burnout and frustration. Holiness is about having our eyes focused singly on Jesus and keeping confidence in him above all others. It's about surrendering to the lordship of the coming King. It's about God working graciously in us to reproduce the beauty of his glorious character in us. The emphasis all the way through is on the work of God. God is the one who sanctifies. God is faithful. God will do it. That's grace.

The second thing that strikes me about this prayer of blessing is the word *entirely*. God is not interested in a little bit of holiness; he's not working to sanctify us in part. He wants to change us through and through, *entirely*, all the way. His project of transformation leaves no part of our lives untouched. That's what Paul means when he talks about the spirit, soul, and body being sound and blameless. He's not telling us about the component parts from which human beings are made. That would be to miss the point. He's telling us that the whole of our being, every aspect of our existence, needs to be transformed and made holy. All of it. Nothing gets left out. God is not satisfied with anything less than everything we've got.

That may sound impossible to you. After all, you know yourself. You know how deep your brokenness runs. You know the hidden places of shame in your life, the self-condemnation you endure. That's why it's essential to stay focused on the word *grace*. You see, Paul knows how deep God's grace penetrates. It will search out the deepest, darkest crevices of our hearts and shine the light of God's holy love into those places. And when that happens, when God fills our worst brokenness with his incomparably beautiful life, we'll discover what it feels like to belong fully to him. And we'll discover what it means to be fully alive.

1. Do you ever find yourself trying to be holy in your own strength? How does that usually work out? What would happen if you began to rely on God's grace?

2. Which areas of your life does God need to transform? Will you yield that to God now?

WEEK FIVE

GATHERING DISCUSSION OUTLINE

A. **Open session in prayer.** Ask that God would astonish us anew with fresh insight from God's Word and transform us into the disciples that Jesus desires us to become.

B. **View video for this week's readings.**

C. **What were key insights or takeaways that you gained from your reading during the week and from watching the video commentary?** In particular, how did these help you to grow in your faith and understanding of Scripture this week? What parts of the Bible lessons or study raised questions for you?

D. **Discuss questions selected from the daily readings.** Invite class members to share key insights or to raise questions that they found to be the most meaningful.

  1. **KEY OBSERVATION:** People should prepare for Jesus' return, not predict its timing.

     DISCUSSION QUESTION: What are concrete ways you can prepare for Jesus' return?

  2. **KEY OBSERVATION:** Christian behavior should reflect Christian identity.

     DISCUSSION QUESTION: In what ways does your sense of self shape your behavior?

3. **KEY OBSERVATION:** Staying faithful and avoiding distraction takes discipline and community.

   DISCUSSION QUESTION: What disciplines are you cultivating to strengthen yourself spiritually?

4. **KEY OBSERVATION:** Community doesn't happen by accident; it takes hard work.

   DISCUSSION QUESTION: How are you actively promoting Christian community?

5. **KEY OBSERVATION:** God's grace can transform us completely.

   DISCUSSION QUESTION: Which area(s) of your life does God need to transform? Will you yield that to God now?

E. **As the study concludes, consider specific ways that this week's Bible lessons invite you to grow and call you to change.** How do this week's scriptures call us to think differently? How do they challenge us to change in order to align ourselves with God's work in the world? What specific actions should we take to apply the insights of the lessons into our daily lives? What kind of person do our Bible lessons call us to become?

F. **Close session with prayer.** Emphasize God's ongoing work of transformation in our lives in preparation for loving mission and service in the world. Pray for absent class members as well as for persons whom we need to invite to join our study.

WEEK SIX

2 Thessalonians 1:1–12

Your Journey toward Glory

ONE

Soon, but Not Now

2 Thessalonians 1:1–2 NIV *Paul, Silas and Timothy,*
To the church of the Thessalonians in God our Father and the Lord Jesus Christ:
²Grace and peace to you from God the Father and the Lord Jesus Christ.

Key Observation. Disciples need grace to admit error and endure.

Understanding the Word. Have you ever known someone with a tendency to take things too far? Perhaps you remember a time you asked a friend or colleague to work on a problem, but once they'd done it you found they'd created a whole new set of problems to be addressed.

The situation in 2 Thessalonians is something like that. We've already learned that one reason Paul wrote 1 Thessalonians was to teach the recipients that Jesus' second coming could happen at any time without warning. In 2 Thessalonians, however, we'll discover that Paul describes various events that he expects to take place before Jesus returns (2:3–12). There's some tension there. And if we could speak with Paul, we may be tempted to ask: Which one is it? Will Jesus come back suddenly with no warning? Or will he return only after some time line has played out?

The good news is that there is a straightforward explanation for what appears to be a different attitude on Paul's part. We'll dig into the details later. For now, consider that Paul wrote to the Thessalonians to instruct them about the future resurrection of the body and the second coming of Jesus. He told them that the second coming of Jesus could happen at any time. He wanted them to be attentive and prepared. But he didn't anticipate the possibility that they might overreact—that they might take his advice too far.

We know the recipients continued to experience persecution (2 Thess. 1:4). Things were tense, and it's possible some of them interpreted some aspect of that conflict as the beginning of God's end-time judgment. They apparently thought the day of the Lord was already in progress (2 Thess. 2:2). Some of them even quit working (2 Thess. 3:11). You may have seen this sort of thing. When a group thinks the end is about to happen, it's common enough for group members to stop everything so they can wait as a group. These things always end in disappointment. Paul told the Thessalonians Jesus could come anytime and some stopped everything (including their work) to watch for it. After all, they're ready to be free of this suffering. They want to be vindicated. But they've taken things a little too far. Paul tells them to get back to work and get on with their lives. The day of Lord has not yet come. There are some things that need to happen first. That doesn't negate what he said in the first letter, it just means the Thessalonians must continue to persevere.

It's no accident that Paul begins this letter (like others) with a wish of grace and peace. Grace and peace are precisely what the recipients will need to admit they were wrong and continue to endure. They're going to need Jesus to empower them and strengthen them and encourage them. And they'll need him to fill their hearts with peace. If he does, they can make it.

1. It takes humility to admit when you're wrong. Think of a time you had to do that. How did that experience shape you?

2. Can you think of a time when Jesus showed grace to you by comforting your heart in a time of suffering? How did that shape your relationship with him?

3. How does unwillingness to confess sin impact our relationship with God and with other people? *Seperates us*
   Pride gets in the way

TWO

Room to Grow

2 Thessalonians 1:3–4 NIV *We ought always to thank God for you, brothers and sisters, and rightly so, because your faith is growing more and more, and the love all of you have for one another is increasing. ⁴Therefore, among God's churches we boast about your perseverance and faith in all the persecutions and trials you are enduring.*

Key Observation. Suffering is an opportunity to become more like Jesus.

Understanding the Word. The difficulties experienced by the believers in Thessalonica haven't gone away. They continue to face persecution. They continue to suffer. We still don't know the exact details. We do know things are tough. Nevertheless, they continue to persevere. The thing to notice is that they are also growing. In fact, Paul names two specific areas of growth—faith and love. You may remember (all the way back in 1 Thessalonians 3:10, 12) that Paul prayed for the Thessalonians in these two areas. He prayed for what was lacking in their faith. And he prayed that they may increase in love. His prayer is, apparently, being answered. That tells us something about the nature of Christian suffering.

It's easy to get discouraged when our faith faces obstacles. Whether the antagonism involves strange looks at our place of employment or physical suffering in a place where Christ is publicly opposed, when things don't go well, we feel defeated. Deflated. Derailed. You can imagine how easy it would've been for the Thessalonians to slide into that mode. But Paul doesn't see it that way. He sees their suffering as something that provides room to grow. Because even though you *feel* like you're losing when you face opposition, you *actually* have an opportunity to become more like Jesus.

Remember that Jesus is the one who suffered for you. He allowed his body to be broken and his blood to be spilled. And he did it because he loves you. His death certainly looked like defeat. The religious leaders and Roman authorities in Judea thought they'd won when Jesus died on the cross. But his suffering was also an expression of his love. And upon his resurrection, it became clear that his suffering was really his victory. Jesus suffered in love for his church and for the world. He did it to make us whole. When you suffer for Jesus, even though it feels like defeat, you need to realize that it's making you more like him. He is our suffering Lord, and he invites us to follow him, and to be like him.

Now that doesn't mean we go looking for trouble. It doesn't mean we should have some sort of martyr complex. It does mean that when trouble presents itself, we look for opportunities to exhibit self-giving, other-oriented, perfect love. Just like Jesus. And chances are our Lord will use it to encourage other communities of faith. That's what Paul means when he mentions his boasting about the Thessalonians to other churches. He knows their example of faithfulness and love will encourage other brothers and sisters in similar struggles. And that's true for you too. So, the next time you face obstacles to faith, work on the discipline of seeing that experience in the shape of the cross.

1. How do seasons of pain shape your trust in Jesus? Has pain tempted you to trust Jesus more or less?

2. Who might benefit from your experience? Who do you know that might be encouraged by your story? Would you be willing to share it with them?

THREE

Is God Just?

2 Thessalonians 1:5–8 NIV *All this is evidence that God's judgment is right, and as a result you will be counted worthy of the kingdom of God, for which you are suffering. ⁶God is just: He will pay back trouble to those who trouble you ⁷and give relief to you who are troubled, and to us as well. This will happen when the Lord Jesus is revealed from heaven in blazing fire with his powerful angels. ⁸He will punish those who do not know God and do not obey the gospel of our Lord Jesus.*

Key Observation. Perseverance is an expression of faith in the justice of God.

Understanding the Word. Is God just? Where is God when his people suffer? Is he paying attention? Does he care? Why doesn't he do something about it?

Questions like these are common when believers suffer. God is supposed to be *our* God. God is supposed to be faithful. God is supposed to be just. And we are hurting. Why doesn't he put a stop to it?

As usual, Paul invites us to see things in a different light. Here he makes the point that faithful endurance in suffering on the part of the Thessalonians is itself evidence of God's righteousness and justice. We're tempted to question God's justice, but Paul reasserts it. What's going on there? Consider that faithful endurance in pain is a way of saying, "I trust you, God." After all, if a believer suffers and falls away, it's evidence that they didn't trust God. They didn't believe he would make things right. Perseverance in pain tells the church and the world that we believe our God will do what he should do. He will act with justice. He will vindicate his people. We'll keep going, because he can be trusted to do what he should.

That's why Paul reminds them that the day will come when God's judgment will be evident to all. Those who afflict the Thessalonians will experience the consequence of their action. And the Thessalonians will be comforted and find relief from their affliction. In the meantime, Paul wants us to remember that suffering produces Christlikeness. Now we've heard that before, and we'll hear it again. It's that important. Jesus suffered. And Jesus invites us to come after him. Staying faithful in the meantime is a way of expressing trust in the ultimate justice of God.

Now you may be thinking, *I've never really had to suffer for Jesus. How does this apply to me?* Well, there are a couple of things you can do. Start by praying for the persecuted church. There are believers all over the world who live in constant danger for following Jesus. Intercede for them. Bear them before God in prayer. Then call attention to their situation. Learn all you can about them and the difficulties they face. Share what you learn with your pastor. Organize teams of people to pray for believers who suffer. Become their advocate. Care for them. They are part of your family of faith; treat them like it. By offering yourself as their advocate, you join them in expressing faith that God will ultimately do justice in their situation.

1. Consider a time when you questioned God's justice. How were your questions resolved? Did that experience change the way you relate to God?

2. What are a few concrete things you can do to support persecuted Christians? When will you start doing them?

3. Think of a time you needed to persevere. How did it impact your relationship with God?

FOUR

Choices Matter

2 Thessalonians 1:9–10 NIV *They will be punished with everlasting destruction and shut out from the presence of the Lord and from the glory of his might* ¹⁰*on the day he comes to be glorified in his holy people and to be marveled at among all those who have believed. This includes you, because you believed our testimony to you.*

Key Observation. Our choices carry real consequences.

Understanding the Word. We all face choices every day. Those choices carry consequences. Sometimes the choices are small and the consequences are trivial. (What will I have for breakfast? What time will I run my errands?) Other times the choices are significant and the consequences have implications for the trajectory of our lives. (Where will I go to school? Should I take this job? Who will I marry?) One of the most substantive choices with the most serious consequences comes in how we respond to the good news that Jesus died for our sin and was raised to give us new life. How will we respond to the news that Jesus is Lord? This is a major choice with massive consequences.

Paul is clear that those who reject the good news of Jesus will suffer grave consequences as a result of that choice. The choice to disobey and disbelieve the gospel leads to the consequence of "everlasting destruction" and separation from God. I know we don't like to talk about that. It makes us uncomfortable; it unsettles us. But we ignore it to our detriment. What will you do with the gospel? What is your attitude toward Jesus? What are the consequences? We need to remember that talk of consequences can be an instrument of God's grace to draw people to Jesus. You may be surprised by what God can do with loving, yet honest, warnings of the danger of rejecting the gospel. Avoiding talk of consequences could undermine the work of God. We certainly don't want to do that.

One other thing. I can't help but think about how some parents are easily tempted to shield their children from the negative consequences of poor choices. We obviously want to protect our kids and we want to give them every opportunity. We don't want them to hurt or feel badly. It could be something small; perhaps failing to discipline a child when he or she is unkind or untruthful. It could be something big. You can probably think of instances in which parents might go to great lengths to keep their children from experiencing the consequences of significant misbehavior. I wonder, however, whether that's really doing our kids a favor or doing them a disservice. If parents shield their children from negative consequences, what does it teach them about God?

We've already seen how Paul wants the Thessalonians to remember that choices have consequences, and sometimes those consequences are severe. That's why he reminds the Thessalonians that those who oppose the gospel and inflict suffering on the church will experience drastic—even disastrous—consequences for those choices. I often remind my kids that I let them face the consequences of their poor decisions because I want them to learn to obey God. I want them to be sensitive to the positive consequences of obeying God and wary of the negative consequences for disobedience.

1. Think of a time you experienced negative consequences for a poor (or sinful) decision. How did those consequences impact you? What did you learn? Did you choose differently the next time?

2. Have you ever shielded another person from negative consequences? How do you think that affected them? Would you do it again? Why?

FIVE

What's the Purpose?

2 Thessalonians 1:11–12 NIV *With this in mind, we constantly pray for you, that our God may make you worthy of his calling, and that by his power he may bring to fruition your every desire for goodness and your every deed prompted by* *faith.* [12] *We pray this so that the name of our Lord Jesus may be glorified in you, and you in him, according to the grace of our God and the Lord Jesus Christ.*

Key Observation. God's grace enables us to embody God's character.

Understanding the Word. I love Paul's prayers. They always take you straight to the point. They are worth reading slowly and carefully. In this instance, Paul is telling the Thessalonians about his habits of prayer on their behalf. And there are two things to notice about it: the petition and the purpose.

The petition is the specific thing (or things) for which Paul is asking. Here he wants the Thessalonians to know that he constantly asks God to empower them to live in a manner worthy of God's call and fill them with resolve. What does it mean to live in a manner worthy of God's call? It means that the character of a person's life reflects favorably on God. You see, God has called his people to be his representatives, to bear his name. When we embody God's character—his faithfulness, his truthfulness, his perfect love—we tell the world the truth about the one we represent. We live worthily of his call. In contrast, when we (as God's representatives) behave in a way that contradicts God's character, we tell the world lies about God. We are not living in a manner worthy of God's call when we misrepresent him to the world.

Paul knows the Thessalonians don't have the power in themselves to do that, so he asks God to work powerfully within them. He asks God to fill them with resolve to be faithful. For the Thessalonians, that means resolve to stand in the face of persecution. For you, it will work out in any number of ways. It will mean resolve to tell the truth when others pressure you to lie. It will mean patience when your children disobey. It will mean keeping your marriage vows. It will mean denying yourself. It will mean embodying self-giving love. Like the Thessalonians, you'll need the power of God, which is exactly what Paul prays for.

The purpose of their faithful resolve is revealed in verse 12. When you see the words "so that," it means Paul is talking about purpose. And the purpose of that resolve is that Christ may be glorified in them. When God's people honor his call and embody his character, it tells the world of the glory of Christ by showing his power to transform rebels into his faithful representatives. What's more, Paul sees a reciprocal relationship at work. When Christ is glorified in us, we are also glorified in him. His desire is to make us participants in all that he is and all that he has. Jesus wants to share his splendor with us. When we are thoroughly surrendered to him, when we offer our lives as one big "yes" to Jesus, he takes us to himself and shares his glory with us. And there is nothing more beautiful than that.

Paul punctuates this prayer report with a reminder that this only happens through God's grace. Never forget that. All the good that we'll ever embody comes as a gift of God's divine grace.

1. Take a moment to consider what sort of things you pray for. How do they compare to Paul's petition that the Thessalonians have faithful resolve? Do you need to change the way you pray?

2. Have you considered that Jesus wants to share his glory with you? What does that tell you about his attitude toward you and others? Do you need to change the way you relate to other people?

3. What aspect of your character needs to better embody God's character?

WEEK SIX

GATHERING DISCUSSION OUTLINE

A. **Open session in prayer.** Ask that God would astonish us anew with fresh insight from God's Word and transform us into the disciples that Jesus desires us to become.

B. **View video for this week's readings.**

C. **What were key insights or takeaways that you gained from your reading during the week and from watching the video commentary?** In particular, how did these help you to grow in your faith and understanding of Scripture this week? What parts of the Bible lessons or study raised questions for you?

D. **Discuss questions selected from the daily readings.** Invite class members to share key insights or to raise questions that they found to be the most meaningful.

   1. **KEY OBSERVATION:** Disciples need grace to admit error and endure.

      DISCUSSION QUESTION: How does unwillingness to confess sin impact our relationship with God and with other people?

   2. **KEY OBSERVATION:** Suffering is an opportunity to become more like Jesus.

      DISCUSSION QUESTION: How do seasons of pain shape your trust in Jesus? Has pain tempted you to trust Jesus more or less?

3. **KEY OBSERVATION:** Perseverance is an expression of faith in the justice of God.

   DISCUSSION QUESTION: Think of a time you needed to persevere. How did it impact your relationship with God?

4. **KEY OBSERVATION:** Our choices carry real consequences.

   DISCUSSION QUESTION: Think of a time you experienced negative consequences for a poor (or sinful) decision. How did those consequences impact you? What did you learn? Did you choose differently the next time?

5. **KEY OBSERVATION:** God's grace enables us to embody God's character.

   DISCUSSION QUESTION: What aspect of your character needs to better embody God's character?

E. **As the study concludes, consider specific ways that this week's Bible lessons invite you to grow and call you to change.** How do this week's scriptures call us to think differently? How do they challenge us to change in order to align ourselves with God's work in the world? What specific actions should we take to apply the insights of the lessons into our daily lives? What kind of person do our Bible lessons call us to become?

F. **Close session with prayer.** Emphasize God's ongoing work of transformation in our lives in preparation for loving mission and service in the world. Pray for absent class members as well as for persons whom we need to invite to join our study.

Praise for conviction
Thank god for making you aware
of your sin

WEEK SEVEN

2 Thessalonians 2:1–17

What Happens Next?

ONE

The Day and Your Identity

2 Thessalonians 2:1–2 *As to the coming of our Lord Jesus Christ and our being gathered together to him, we beg you, brothers and sisters, ²not to be quickly shaken in mind or alarmed, either by spirit or by word or by letter, as though from us, to the effect that the day of the Lord is already here.*

Key Observation. Trusting Jesus guards us against unnecessary anxiety.

Understanding the Word. This is where we discover Paul's main reason for writing this letter. The recipients have heard reports that the day of the Lord has already begun, and Paul is writing to correct that false information.

Now you may wonder how they could think such a thing. After all, Paul's description of that day in 1 Thessalonians 4:13–5:11 portrays it as a very public, very obvious, world-shaking event. Jesus is supposed to return with trumpets sounding and angels shouting. How could the Thessalonians mistake that? People consumed with end-time scenarios often interpret the smallest events to have cosmic significance. It could be that some sort of local crisis happened in Thessalonica and some in the community interpreted that as the beginning of the judgment against their opponents and then things just got out of hand. Paul found himself confronted with a situation in which people who weren't anticipating the day of the Lord (perhaps only weeks before!) now think it's already begun. With this new situation, it's no wonder 2 Thessalonians has a somewhat different feel than 1 Thessalonians.

Now you may be wondering how this bad information could have infiltrated the community, and it's not clear that Paul knows. He mentions that it could have come "by spirit or by word or by letter." The language of "spirit" may refer to someone's word of prophecy; "word" could refer to a sermon or message from some unnamed person (e.g., a traveling preacher); the "letter" option would mean someone wrote a letter and signed Paul's name to it. However the news came to Thessalonica, Paul wants them to know it's inaccurate. The day of the Lord has not yet come.

You get a feel for Paul's sense of urgency when he says "we beg you." He takes this seriously. One reason may be that the community itself is defined in terms of the day of the Lord. Remember that he called them "children of the day" in 1 Thessalonians 5:5. Their shared sense of identity is bound up in their anticipation of the day. If they get false information about that, then it could shake the foundations of the community—chip away at their identity. The health and stability of the community is at stake. If they are going to remain unshaken, they need to keep their eyes on Jesus as they await the day of the Lord. If they stay focused on Jesus and avoid unnecessary alarm about local rumblings, they will be positioned to continue in faithful perseverance.

1. Have you ever encountered a significant event that fundamentally reshaped your sense of self? How would you describe that experience?

2. How might things be different if your identity is primarily defined by Jesus and the knowledge that he will one day return?

3. What makes you anxious? What would it take to be free from that?

Phillipians 4:6   *The climate of the world today*

TWO

The Lawless One

2 Thessalonians 2:3–5 *Let no one deceive you in any way; for that day will not come unless the rebellion comes first and the lawless one is revealed, the one destined for destruction. ⁴He opposes and exalts himself above every so-called god or object of worship, so that he takes his seat in the temple of God, declaring himself to be God. ⁵Do you not remember that I told you these things when I was still with you?*

Key Observation. Watch out for counterfeit gods.

Understanding the Word. Paul now introduces a new character and we wish he'd told us even more, because what we get is somewhat vague. We don't get a name and we don't get a specific time about this person's arrival. Maybe the recipients already had some of the details. After all, Paul mentions that he told them about "these things" before. He may not have felt the need to add detail about someone the congregation was already familiar with.

So what do we know? For starters, Paul calls this fellow "the lawless one" and "the one destined for destruction." Then he describes a series of actions this lawless one will take. He will exalt himself as an object of worship, use the temple as the place of that worship, and even declare himself to be God. In other words, he's a counterfeit, so don't be fooled.

Now I want to urge some caution regarding the identity of this figure. Many have speculated about his identity. Some think he is the antichrist spoken of elsewhere in the Bible. I'm very hesitant to use that language because Paul doesn't use that language. The term "antichrist" comes from 1 John 2:18, 22; 4:3; and 2 John 7. And John's use of antichrist language doesn't quite match Paul's description of the lawless one. For example, Paul describes a single figure—one person. First John mentions a plurality of antichrists (2:18). Beyond that, John describes people who are former members of the community he's writing to (1 John 2:19). Paul gives no hint that this lawless one will arise out of the Christian community. Paul and John are dealing with two different topics. Let's not conflate them.

So, if we can't nail down the identity of this figure, what do we do with this passage of Scripture? I suggest we spend time thinking about counterfeits and pay attention to the command that opens verse 3: don't be deceived. Counterfeits are fundamentally deceptive. They aren't the real thing, but they're designed to make you think they are. Now if you want to be able to spot a counterfeit, you don't want to spend all your time looking at the counterfeits. After all, there could be an infinite number of variations. No, if you want to be able to identify a counterfeit, you need to spend all your time focused on the one real thing—the thing the counterfeit is imitating. And in this case, the real thing is Jesus.

A lot of people spend a lot of time trying to identify the various end-time figures in the Bible. Who is the man of lawlessness? Can we figure it out? Does this person fit the description? Does that one? Wouldn't it be better, though, to use all that time differently? Wouldn't it be better to spend that time focused on the reality instead of the counterfeit? Wouldn't it be better to focus on Jesus? Of course it would. If you spend your time growing in knowledge and love of Jesus, you probably won't have any trouble identifying false gods when they present themselves.

1. What sorts of things distract you from Jesus?

2. What can you do today to refocus yourself on Jesus?

3. What are the counterfeit gods in our society? In your life?

THREE

Jesus Wins

2 Thessalonians 2:6–8 *And you know what is now restraining him, so that he may be revealed when his time comes. ⁷For the mystery of lawlessness is already at work, but only until the one who now restrains it is removed. ⁸And then the lawless one will be revealed, whom the Lord Jesus will destroy with the breath of his mouth, annihilating him by the manifestation of his coming.*

Key Observation. Evil is a powerful force, but Jesus wins in the end.

Understanding the Word. The next new character we meet is the restrainer. It turns out that Paul's description of this figure is even more vague than was his description of the lawless one. It's not even clear that the restrainer is a person. Note the way Paul begins verse 6 saying, "*what* is now restraining" (emphasis added) only to shift his language in verse 7 to "*the one who* now restrains" (emphasis added). Is the restrainer a thing or a person? We simply don't know. Apparently, the Thessalonians did. Paul says as much at the beginning of 2:6. He had spoken with them about this before, so they had more information than we do. That means caution is warranted—some interpretive restraint, perhaps. Despite the need for caution, plenty of people speculate about the identity of this restrainer. Some think the restrainer is the Roman

Empire with its laws that keep society in order. Others think Paul is referring to demonic powers. Still others think the restrainer is God. And then there's a group that sees the proclamation of the gospel as the restraining force. In reality, we simply lack the necessary evidence to make a judgment about the identity of the restrainer. Whoever (or whatever) it is, it will eventually be removed and the lawless one will be unveiled. Then the day of the Lord will come and Jesus will defeat the lawless one. And that brings us to a key point in this passage: Jesus wins!

Remember that Paul's desire is to reduce anxiety among the recipients. He doesn't want the community shaken by uncertainty regarding the future, so he reminds them of what is most certain: Jesus wins in the end. Yes, evil is powerful. Yes, the people of God may suffer for a season. Yes, it *feels* like the world is in chaos. Nevertheless, the Lord Jesus Christ reigns on the throne of heaven and he will one day return and put an end to every force of evil. No exceptions.

Pay attention to the way Paul describes the victory. Jesus will destroy the lawless one with his breath. It's almost anticlimactic. There's no great battle. There's no big confrontation. Jesus just wins. That's it. And that's a good reminder that evil (or Satan) is not an equal and opposite force to God. Demons are not infinite in power. They do not know everything. They do not have the ability to be everywhere. They aren't gods. The lawless one is a rebellious *creature*. Jesus is the Creator. The Creator does not struggle against his creatures. They have no potential to overthrow their Maker. God is infinite in power. Evil is not. All Jesus does is show up. Reveal himself. Breathe. And he wins. Evil doesn't stand a chance. Remember that.

1. A lot of people grow anxious over end-time scenarios and attempts to identify end-time figures. How does the knowledge of Jesus' infinite power impact your attitude toward the future?

2. Have you ever been in a situation where evil seemed unstoppable? How would you describe that? How does the ultimate victory of Jesus shape your experience of evil?

3. How can Christian communities point the world to the ultimate victory of Jesus?

FOUR

Deception and Delusion

2 Thessalonians 2:9–12 *The coming of the lawless one is apparent in the working of Satan, who uses all power, signs, lying wonders, [10]and every kind of wicked deception for those who are perishing, because they refused to love the truth and so be saved. [11]For this reason God sends them a powerful delusion, leading them to believe what is false, [12]so that all who have not believed the truth but took pleasure in unrighteousness will be condemned.*

Key Observation. Be on guard against the deceptive power of evil.

Understanding the Word. Have you ever watched a movie only to find yourself cheering for the wrong person? Maybe it's a story about a couple whose marriage is struggling. One of the spouses meets someone new. The new relationship is portrayed positively. The spouse is framed as the enemy of happiness. Before you know it, you're rooting for the marriage to fail and the adulterous relationship to succeed. I hope you see that for what it is: the deceptive power of evil. God is never okay with infidelity. The promise of happiness in that story is a lie, but the power of those stories is a good reminder that evil is always deceptive and we're easily manipulated into loving what God hates.

Paul wants the Thessalonians to understand that too. They must guard against the deceptive influence of evil. Because when the lawless one comes, he will put on a spectacular show. Paul mentions powers, signs, and wonders. But those wonders are *lying* wonders. That power is *deceptive* power. In reality, the power of Satan stands behind the lawless one. That may not be apparent when the time comes, but Paul urgently wants to protect his readers from the deception. Don't be taken in. Remember we are dealing with a counterfeit here. If you want to stay safe, stay focused on the real thing. Stay focused on Jesus.

There are two other observations to make. Both are important. Both are unsettling. First, the alternative to loving God is loving sin. Paul mentions those who take pleasure in unrighteousness. These folks enjoy their opposition to God. They probably don't think of it that way. Let's return to the movie analogy. Some people will keep watching the movie, even though they know it's cultivating desires that God opposes. We easily rationalize the choice. *Oh, it's just a movie. It's just harmless entertainment.* But is it? Attempts to justify sin punctuate our delusion. We are choosing to love unrighteousness, not the righteous one.

Second, the longer we give ourselves to sin, the harder it is to come back. That's the point when Paul mentions how God sends a powerful delusion to those who choose unrighteousness. That statement may be off-putting. Would God really work to increase a person's delusion? The idea here is similar to what we find in Romans 1:24–28, where Paul repeatedly says that God gives people over to the depravity they choose. We need to understand that when we choose sin over holiness, God gives us what we ask for. When we allow ourselves to be entertained by stories that glorify adultery (or other sins), what happens to our patterns of thinking? How does it shape our attitude toward our own marriage? Stories are powerful. And if we continually submit ourselves to stories that undermine God's best, we will cultivate habits that prefer sin to God. We cultivate the delusion. And we'll be getting what we asked for. Sin is habitual. And the longer we give ourselves to unholy habits, the harder it is to come back.

1. Think of a time when the deceptive power of evil was particularly apparent. How would you describe it?

2. Is there something in your life that you know is wrong, yet you still run to it? How would you describe it? What can you do now to change? Who can help you?

3. What is the most subtle expression of evil you can think of? How can Christians guard against that?

FIVE

Made for Glory

2 Thessalonians 2:13–17 *But we must always give thanks to God for you, brothers and sisters beloved by the Lord, because God chose you as the first fruits for salvation through sanctification by the Spirit and through belief in the truth.* [14]*For this purpose he called you through our proclamation of the good news, so that you may obtain the glory of our Lord Jesus Christ.* [15]*So then, brothers and*

sisters, stand firm and hold fast to the traditions that you were taught by us, either by word of mouth or by our letter.
¹⁶Now may our Lord Jesus Christ himself and God our Father, who loved us and through grace gave us eternal comfort and good hope, ¹⁷comfort your hearts and strengthen them in every good work and word.

Key Observation. God made you for glory, but you must stand firm.

Understanding the Word. What does it mean to be human? How do human beings flourish? What does wholeness look like? Those questions are deeply relevant to these final verses in 2 Thessalonians. Here Paul offers a vision of human life as it should be—as God desires it to be.

The focus here is on God's choice: *God chose you.* The question is: What did he choose you for? Paul starts with sanctification. Or, put differently, holiness. Holiness is about human beings coming to embody the character of God more and more. How do we become holy? Paul highlights two instruments necessary for our sanctification: the Holy Spirit and commitment to truth. The Holy Spirit is God's personal presence with, in, and among his people. And if you want to understand the primary work of the Spirit, the answer is only one word: *holiness.* The Holy Spirit wants to cultivate God's holy character in you. That means holiness only happens through God's power. We don't have the strength or ability to make ourselves holy. Only God through his Spirit can do that. He initiates the process.

But that doesn't mean we're not involved. That's why Paul adds the part about believing the truth. This whole chapter has been about unmasking deception. Paul illumined the lie that the day of the Lord has already come (2:2–3). He pointed to the deception that comes from the lawless one (2:9–10). He describes the deceptive power of evil in general. Now he gives us the antidote to deception: believe the truth. Truth is found in Jesus; he's the reality that the lawless one will try to counterfeit. Believing the truth means focusing on Jesus. The Holy Spirit wants to cultivate single-minded devotion to Jesus in you. If you don't resist that, the truth of Jesus will characterize your life. You will be true. You will be holy.

The ultimate goal of that process is participation in the glory of Christ. The theme of human glory came up in 2 Thessalonians 1:12. Now we find it again. And here's what you need to know. There is nothing more beautiful than the glory of the perfect love that exists eternally between God the Father, God the Son, and God the Holy Spirit. The amazing thing is that God invites us to participate in the beauty of the glory of that perfect love. And that, my friends, is what it means to be fully human. That is God's best for human life. Perfect, whole, complete participation in God's unfailing love. That is what God wants for you. Sin keeps us from that. Paul urgently encourages his readers to stand firm and hold on to the truth. Because you don't want to miss God's best. And God's best is participation in his perfect love.

1. Take a moment to reflect on the beauty of God's perfect love. Now consider how often we choose sin instead of God's love. Why do you think we do that? How can Christian community help us change?

2. Think about an advertisement you've recently encountered. How did that ad portray full human life? How is that different from the wholeness described in this passage?

3. What does it mean to be human?

WEEK SEVEN

GATHERING DISCUSSION OUTLINE

A. **Open session in prayer.** Ask that God would astonish us anew with fresh insight from God's Word and transform us into the disciples that Jesus desires us to become.

B. **View video for this week's readings.**

C. **What were key insights or takeaways that you gained from your reading during the week and from watching the video commentary?** In particular, how did these help you to grow in your faith and understanding of Scripture this week? What parts of the Bible lessons or study raised questions for you?

D. **Discuss questions selected from the daily readings.** Invite class members to share key insights or to raise questions that they found to be the most meaningful.

Matthew 6:25-34

1. **KEY OBSERVATION:** Trusting Jesus guards us against unnecessary anxiety. *Isaiah 40:39* *Proverbs* *Psalms 34*

    DISCUSSION QUESTION: What makes you anxious? What would it take to be free from that? *health of family, work, kids, spouse, finances*

2. **KEY OBSERVATION:** Watch out for counterfeit gods.

    DISCUSSION QUESTION: What are the counterfeit gods in our society? In your life? *work, social media, tv*

3. **KEY OBSERVATION:** Evil is a powerful force, but Jesus wins in the end.

DISCUSSION QUESTION: How can Christian communities point the world to the ultimate victory of Jesus?

4. **KEY OBSERVATION:** Be on guard against the deceptive power of evil.

   DISCUSSION QUESTION: What is the most subtle expression of evil you can think of? How can Christians guard against that?

5. **KEY OBSERVATION:** God made you for glory, but you must stand firm.

   DISCUSSION QUESTION: What does it mean to be human?

   John 3:16   Corinthians 13   1 John 4:8

E. **As the study concludes, consider specific ways that this week's Bible lessons invite you to grow and call you to change.** How do this week's scriptures call us to think differently? How do they challenge us to change in order to align ourselves with God's work in the world? What specific actions should we take to apply the insights of the lessons into our daily lives? What kind of person do our Bible lessons call us to become?

F. **Close session with prayer.** Emphasize God's ongoing work of transformation in our lives in preparation for loving mission and service in the world. Pray for absent class members as well as for persons whom we need to invite to join our study.

2 Thessalonians 3:1–18

Wrapping Up

ONE

Driven by Passion

2 Thessalonians 3:1–2 NIV *As for other matters, brothers and sisters, pray for us that the message of the Lord may spread rapidly and be honored, just as it was with you. ²And pray that we may be delivered from wicked and evil people, for not everyone has faith.*

Key Observation. Passion for Jesus overflows in prayer and mission.

Understanding the Word. Most of us tend to talk about the people and things we love. Consider a grandmother who can't wait to tell you about her grandchildren. Or a husband eager to brag on his wife. Maybe you know someone who talks mostly about college football. Or hunting. Or politics. People talk about their passions. How often do we talk to people about Jesus and the gospel? What does that say about our passion?

If his letters are any indication, Paul was deeply passionate about Jesus. He preached about Jesus. He wrote about Jesus. He devoted his life to cultivating communities centered on Jesus. He was all about the spread of the gospel. And he didn't just want the gospel to spread. He wanted the gospel to spread *rapidly*. And he invited others to join the mission. Here Paul invites the Thessalonians to share in the mission to spread the gospel—the Word of the Lord—by praying for him and his coworkers. He wants the Thessalonians to intercede for him before God. They've experienced the fruit of the gospel in their community, now it's time for them to help cultivate the gospel elsewhere. One way for the recipients to take an active part in Paul's work is prayer. And the more they pray for Paul, the more they become deeply invested in the mission. Prayer takes time. Serious prayer takes serious commitment. That's what Paul wants from the Thessalonian believers.

So, what does he want them to pray for? There are people out there who do not want to acknowledge the lordship of Jesus. Sadly, they have no interest in his self-giving love. More than that, Paul understands that the gospel faces opposition. There are some who don't merely reject the good news of Jesus, they are overtly antagonistic to it. People like that may even be willing to inflict suffering on people like Paul. Now the Thessalonians should be able to sympathize. We've seen again and again how they suffered for their faith. Surely, they'll be eager to pray for Paul's rescue from faithless people. Their readiness to devote serious energy in prayer for Paul will correspond to the depth of their passion for the gospel.

What are you doing to spread the gospel? Do other people see your passion for Jesus? Perhaps you'll consider accepting Paul's invitation: make time to pray for the mission. Pray for your church. Pray for your pastor, as he or she leads your church in mission. Pray that obstacles to the gospel will be removed. Pray that missionaries will have fruitful ministry. Invest yourself in prayer. It will change you. It will form you. It will reproduce the passions of Jesus in you. And make time to talk to others about Jesus. Give them a chance to see your passion.

1. How would you describe your prayer life? How do you feel about prayer? Enthusiastic? Anxious? Something else? What would it look like to take the next step in the discipline of prayer?

2. When was the last time you told someone about Jesus? Who will you tell next?

3. What are you doing to cultivate passion for Jesus?

Prayer
walks w/ gospel music
Grace Place

TWO
Faithful Lord, Faithful People

2 Thessalonians 3:3–5 NIV *But the Lord is faithful, and he will strengthen you and protect you from the evil one. ⁴We have confidence in the Lord that you are doing and will continue to do the things we command. ⁵May the Lord direct your hearts into God's love and Christ's perseverance.*

Key Observation. Perseverance in faith is built on the faithfulness of Jesus.

Understanding the Word. If you were writing to a group of suffering believers, how would you wrap up the letter? What would you say to encourage them to keep going despite difficulty? Where would you point them? Paul invites the troubled Thessalonians to look to Jesus. And the chief aspect of our Lord's character that's in focus is his faithfulness. Jesus is faithful. That's the most important thing to remember in times of suffering. No matter how bad it seems. Now matter how hard it gets. Jesus is faithful.

Because Jesus is faithful, the Thessalonians can count on him to strengthen them in their struggle. Perhaps you know what they feel like. Weak. Exhausted. Afraid. Confused. They were unsettled by reports that the day of the Lord had already come (2:2). They faced opposition. Some had given up work. It probably seemed as if the whole world stood against them. My guess is that you've felt that way at one time or another. Paul wants them (and you!) to count on Jesus to protect you. So he articulates an aspect of the doctrine of *assurance*. That doctrine tells us that you don't have to wonder whether Jesus loves you. You don't have to wonder whether he'll ever give up on you. Friends and family will disappoint you. Other believers will let you down. Jesus will not abandon you—ever.

The thing to see is that assurance is essential for perseverance. The knowledge of Christ's faithfulness should empower the Thessalonians (and you!) to remain faithful. And faithfulness is not about holding on in the short-term. Following Jesus isn't a sprint. It's more like a marathon. It takes endurance. It takes long-term commitment. And it's not easy. There's a reason Paul mentions the "evil one" here. Believers will face antagonism and opposition, but that opposition is never too much for Jesus. That's why Paul is confident they will stand firm. If they keep their eyes on Jesus, they'll have what they need to stay the course.

Let me say a little more about Paul's mention of the "evil one." What does it mean that he mentions Satan in the context of describing the believer's assurance and perseverance? This is a good reminder that Satan is not equal to Jesus—not in terms of power, knowledge, or presence. The evil one is finite and limited. Yes, he's powerful, but he's no match for Christ. He's a creature. Jesus is the Creator. Believers will undoubtedly face seasons of life in which it *feels* as if the enemy is winning. It's essential to remember he's not. Jesus is able to guard you. Not even Satan can steal the believer's assurance of God's love in Christ.

1. Think of time you were discouraged in your Christian journey. How would you describe that experience? How does the knowledge of Christ's unfailing love transform that experience?

2. Paul expresses love for the Thessalonians by reminding them of Jesus' unfailing love. What are some specific ways you can express that love? How can you embody the faithfulness of Jesus to other believers?

3. How has Jesus shown faithfulness to you?

Bringing people that I need in my life
Grace Place
Answered prayer

THREE

Faithful Work

2 Thessalonians 3:6–12 NIV *In the name of the Lord Jesus Christ, we command you, brothers and sisters, to keep away from every believer who is idle and disruptive and does not live according to the teaching you received from us. [7]For you yourselves know how you ought to follow our example. We were not idle when we were with you, [8]nor did we eat anyone's food without paying for it. On the contrary, we worked night and day, laboring and toiling so that we would not be a burden to any of you. [9]We did this, not because we do not have the right to such help, but in order to offer ourselves as a model for you to imitate. [10]For even when we were with you, we gave you this rule: "The one who is unwilling to work shall not eat."*

¹¹We hear that some among you are idle and disruptive. They are not busy; they are busybodies. ¹²Such people we command and urge in the Lord Jesus Christ to settle down and earn the food they eat.

Key Observation. Work is essential to cultivating Christian community.

Understanding the Word. We don't know with certainty why some of the Thessalonians had given up working. It's possible the problem was related to their confusion about the return of Jesus. If Jesus is coming back at any moment, why keep working? For Paul, however, that's an unacceptable conclusion. Work is essential for cultivating Christian community. And to deal with these folks, Paul needs to instruct the church in two areas: (1) the theology of work and (2) church discipline. We'll handle the first today and the second tomorrow.

Paul's theology of work is really about self-giving love. Notice the way he describes his work among the Thessalonians: "we worked night and day, laboring and toiling so that we would not be a burden to any of you" (2 Thess. 3:8 NIV; see the similar point in 1 Thessalonians 2:9). When Paul was living among the Thessalonians, he also worked alongside them. He believed that apostles had the right to not work and still be supported by the church, but he chose not to exercise that right (2 Thess. 3:9). Instead, he wanted to carry his own weight in order to avoid adding extra burdens to the young church. Notice Paul's motivation. He loves them. He wants them to grow in faith. He doesn't want to create hindrances to their growth. So, he chooses to forego his rights and support himself. This is an expression of his love for the congregation. Now Paul wants the Thessalonians to imitate his example of love.

Not only is work an expression of love toward other believers, it's also a means for strengthening the church. For many, a job is an end in itself. They live for their work. Everything else takes second place. Paul sees things differently. Work is important, but glorifying Jesus by strengthening the church is ultimate. Work should be a means to that end. Take a minute to imagine what it would be like if followers of Jesus saw their jobs as a means to meet their needs *so that* they can participate deeply in the advance of the kingdom of God. Work is clearly a necessity. The question is whether we work to get more stuff or whether we work to give more to Jesus and build up the church.

When we see work in these ways, it becomes clear that the nonworking idle members of the Thessalonian community are focused on themselves and their preferences rather than relieving the burdens of the community. They aren't expressing self-giving love. They aren't embodying the character of Jesus. Their attitude toward work is a threat to a community that is already struggling. If they don't change, there will be consequences. We'll tackle that tomorrow.

1. In your experience, how do people tend to see their job? Do they live to work? Or do they work in order to strengthen the church?

2. How would your life be different if your job was a means to the end of strengthening the church?

3. How does your work relate to your Christian vocation?

FOUR

Tough Love

2 Thessalonians 3:6–12 NIV *In the name of the Lord Jesus Christ, we command you, brothers and sisters, to keep away from every believer who is idle and disruptive and does not live according to the teaching you received from us. [7]For you yourselves know how you ought to follow our example. We were not idle when we were with you, [8]nor did we eat anyone's food without paying for it. On the contrary, we worked night and day, laboring and toiling so that we would not be a burden to any of you. [9]We did this, not because we do not have the right to such help, but in order to offer ourselves as a model for you to imitate. [10]For even when we were with you, we gave you this rule: "The one who is unwilling to work shall not eat."*

[11]We hear that some among you are idle and disruptive. They are not busy; they are busybodies. [12]Such people we command and urge in the Lord Jesus Christ to settle down and earn the food they eat.

Key Observation. The goal of church discipline is restoration, not removal.

Understanding the Word. Many people recoil at the language of church discipline. It feels mean, so we avoid it. But Paul didn't avoid it, and neither did Jesus (see Matthew 18:15–17). In this passage, the apostle plainly instructs the Thessalonians to break fellowship with those who refuse to work. This is an expression of church discipline. We need to shift our thinking about church discipline. It's not a matter of being mean or unkind. It's an expression of love. Here's what I mean.

The idle among the Thessalonians are a threat to the health of the congregation. Think about it. The Thessalonians are suffering antagonism from their neighbors. They live with instability, fear, and anxiety. These idle ones are taking a bad situation and making it worse by increasing the burden on others who must make up for the lost work. Thus, by offering this word of correction, Paul expresses love to the church. He takes the burden of disciplining those who threaten the well-being of the community. If his efforts are effective, the desperate situation will be somewhat more stable.

Paul's insistence on discipline is also an expression of love to the idle. They are sinning against their brothers and sisters, and that sin is detrimental to their own spiritual health. They cannot experience God's best while they are harming God's church. By initiating a process of discipline, Paul is doing what is sometimes called "tough love." He's willing to have the hard conversation because he knows it's for the best.

There are two forms of church discipline. I like to call them *formative discipline* and *corrective discipline*. Formative discipline has to do with training and education. It's the kind of discipline athletes cultivate during practice. It happens through deep and long-term engagement with Scripture, prayer, worship, serving, and participating in mission. When you engage in these disciplines, the character of Christ is formed in you.

But there's also corrective discipline. And that's what Paul is doing here. Corrective discipline addresses a problem or identifies a danger, then a process of reconciliation is put in place. Hopefully, the folks who need correcting will repent. If they do, they are restored to the community. It's absolutely essential to remember what we previously said: corrective discipline is an expression of love. It's all about helping a person find their way back to God's best.

The last point to be made is that corrective discipline comes with the goal of restoration. This point is missed too often. Paul's aim here is not to punish or exact retribution. He's trying to put pressure on the idle to bring them back into a healthy relationship with the community. Notice the last verse. Paul commands the idle to get back to work. If they repent and do that, then they are reconciled to God and to the others. The goal isn't removal; it's peace.

1. How would you respond if you were subjected to corrective church discipline?

2. How can the community of believers cultivate healthy and accountable formative discipline?

3. How would you go about correcting someone with love whose behavior is a risk to the community?

Follow the holy spirit

FIVE

Persevere in Peace

2 Thessalonians 3:13–18 NIV *And as for you, brothers and sisters, never tire of doing what is good.*

14Take special note of anyone who does not obey our instruction in this letter. Do not associate with them, in order that they may feel ashamed. 15Yet do not regard them as an enemy, but warn them as you would a fellow believer.

16Now may the Lord of peace himself give you peace at all times and in every way. The Lord be with all of you.

17I, Paul, write this greeting in my own hand, which is the distinguishing mark in all my letters. This is how I write.

18The grace of our Lord Jesus Christ be with you all.

Key Observation. Ultimate peace only comes through the grace of Jesus Christ.

Understanding the Word. Weariness is a danger when perseverance is required. As Paul concludes this second letter to the believers in Thessalonica, he focuses on their need to stand firm. He knows the temptations they'll face. He knows they could easily grow tired in the battle to endure—day after day after day. They must be vigilant. They must guard the gospel and each other.

This letter is primarily about correcting errors. One error was the claim that the day of the Lord had already come. Another error came in the refusal of some to work and so share the burdens of the community. It's no surprise that Paul uses these concluding thoughts to remind the recipients to be vigilant with regard to correcting error. It's easy to see how important this is for Paul. He's willing to break fellowship over it. That's always lamentable, but it's necessary at times. We must also remember, though, that separation is not Paul's ultimate goal. That's why he says to regard them as believers, not enemies. Paul's hope is that pressure from the community will lead those in error to repent.

The goal is peace. Paul's makes that clear by repeating that word—"may the Lord of *peace* himself give you *peace* at all times and in every way" (3:16 NIV, emphasis added). That's what Paul wants. He wants this strife-racked community to be at peace. That only comes with the presence of Jesus. And it only comes if they vigilantly care for one another. That means building up one another. But it also means correcting those who threaten the community with false teaching (i.e., the day of the Lord has come) and selfish practices (i.e., idleness). Peace will flourish only when believers are singly focused on Jesus and care more for each other than they do themselves. That's Paul's hope for the Thessalonians. That's my hope for you.

Did you notice that Paul begins and ends this letter with the twin themes of grace and peace? That's no accident. The apostle knows that the goal of peace can only be achieved by means of God's grace given through Jesus. Authentic Christian peace is not something we can muster up. Jesus makes peace between us and God. Jesus makes peace between Christian brothers and sisters. Take a moment to imagine what it would be like for churches to consistently embody that sort of deep peace. Would it change the church? Would it change the world? That's Paul's vision. Let's make it ours.

1. Is there anyone with whom you need to make peace? When will you do it?

2. How does confronting sin among believers encourage peace in the church?

3. What can you do to make peace in a setting of strife?

WEEK EIGHT

GATHERING DISCUSSION OUTLINE

A. **Open session in prayer.** Ask that God would astonish us anew with fresh insight from God's Word and transform us into the disciples that Jesus desires us to become.

B. **View video for this week's readings.**

C. **What were key insights or takeaways that you gained from your reading during the week and from watching the video commentary?** In particular, how did these help you to grow in your faith and understanding of Scripture this week? What parts of the Bible lessons or study raised questions for you?

D. **Discuss questions selected from the daily readings.** Invite class members to share key insights or to raise questions that they found to be the most meaningful.

1. **KEY OBSERVATION:** Passion for Jesus overflows in prayer and mission.

    DISCUSSION QUESTION: What are you doing to cultivate passion for Jesus?

2. **KEY OBSERVATION:** Perseverance in faith is built on the faithfulness of Jesus.

    DISCUSSION QUESTION: How has Jesus shown faithfulness to you?

3. **KEY OBSERVATION:** Work is essential to cultivating Christian community.

DISCUSSION QUESTION: How does your work relate to your Christian vocation?

4. **KEY OBSERVATION:** The goal of church discipline is restoration, not removal.

   DISCUSSION QUESTION: How would you go about correcting someone with love whose behavior is a risk to the community?

5. **KEY OBSERVATION:** Ultimate peace only comes through the grace of Jesus Christ.

   DISCUSSION QUESTION: What can you do to make peace in a setting of strife?

E. **As the study concludes, consider specific ways that this week's Bible lessons invite you to grow and call you to change.** How do this week's scriptures call us to think differently? How do they challenge us to change in order to align ourselves with God's work in the world? What specific actions should we take to apply the insights of the lessons into our daily lives? What kind of person do our Bible lessons call us to become?

F. **Close session with prayer.** Emphasize God's ongoing work of transformation in our lives in preparation for loving mission and service in the world. Express gratitude for the journey of the past eight weeks through the letters to the Thessalonians.

Women in the New Testament
   March